MUSTANG BON FOUNDATION

These advanced practices should only be practiced after getting the appropriate transmission, and done only by practitioners with appropriate qualifications, permissions, and pith instructions. Without such qualifications, permissions, and instructions these practices can be dangerous, so do not put yourself at risk.

The Twenty-One Nails: According to the Zhang Zhung Oral Transmission Lineage of Bon Dzogchen

ISBN: 978-1-956950-06-9
Library of Congress Control Number: 2019916795

Published by Mustang Bon Publishing

Second Edition

Front cover: Tapihritsa (photograph of thangka taken by Gary Freeman)

MustangBonFoundation.org

Printed and Bound in the United States of America

Layout and design by Brad Reynolds integralartandstudies.com

The Twenty-One Nails

TAPIHRITSA
8th CENTURY C.E.

THE TWENTY-ONE NAILS
ACCORDING TO THE ZHANG ZHUNG
ORAL TRANSMISSION LINEAGE OF
BON DZOGCHEN

ROOT TEXT BY
TAPIHRITSA

AUTO-COMMENTARY ATTRIBUTED TO
GYERPUNG NANGZHER LODPO

TRANSLATED UNDER THE GUIDANCE OF
HIS HOLINESS THE THIRTY-THIRD
MENRI TRIZIN

BY GESHE SONAM GURUNG AND DANIEL P. BROWN, PH.D.

FOR MUSTANG BON FOUNDATION

MUSTANG BON
FOUNDATION

May the translation of these precious lineage teachings
cause their benefits to flourish everywhere
and serve the welfare of all beings.

Geshe Sonam Gurung grew up in an indigenous Bon Tibetan region of Nepal, in the Pangling Village area of Central Mustang. When he was nine years old he was sent by the local Bon lama to become a monk at Menri Monastery, the seat of the indigenous Bon religion, now located in the Dolanji area of India. He spent fourteen years obtaining his Geshe degree (the equivalent of a doctoral degree in Bon spiritual studies) under the guidance of His Holiness Menri Trizin, the spiritual leader and lineage holder of the Bon and the 33rd Head Abbott of Menri Monastery. After obtaining his Geshe degree he served as treasurer, guest master, and personal assistant to His Holiness Menri Trizin at Menri Monastery. Recently, Geshe Sonam returned to the Jomsom area of Central Mustang to reestablish and spread the indigenous Bon teachings in his country of origin. Two documentaries have been made about Geshe Sonam's life and work: *Bon: From Mustang to Menri*, and a follow-up film about his return home, *Returning the Blessings*.

Daniel P. Brown, Ph.D. is an Associate Clinical Professor in Psychology, Dept. of Psychiatry, at Harvard Medical School at Beth Israel Deaconess Medical Center. He teaches a variety of clinical assessment and treatment courses and also a course on performance excellence for physicians, CEOs, and judges. In graduate school at the University of Chicago he studied Sanskrit, and at the University of Wisconsin he studied Tibetan, Buddhist Sanskrit, and Pali. In the 1980s he wrote *Transformations of Consciousness* with Ken Wilber and Jack Engler. He is also the author of *Pointing Out the Great Way: The Stages of Meditation in the Mahamudra Tradition*. More recently, under the guidance of H.H. Menri Trizin, he and Geshe Sonam translated Bru rGyal ba g.Yung drung's *The Pith Instructions for the Stages of the Practice Sessions of Bon rDzogs Chen [Great Completion] Meditation*, and a collection of eleven advanced yogic texts, Shar rdza bKra' shis rGyal mtshan's *sKu gsum rang shar [Self-Arising Three-fold Embodiment of Enlightenment]*.

Table of Contents

THE TWENTY-ONE NAILS
ACCORDING TO THE ZHANG ZHUNG ORAL
TRANSMISSION LINEAGE OF BON DZOGCHEN

Table of Contents

Acknowledgments

Our deepest appreciation to His Holiness the 33rd Menri Trizin, who gave us permission to re-translate this work with a set of technical terms consistent with the other translations we have published. Also, deepest gratitude to Susan Pottish for her thorough and careful copy editing of this manuscript. Our deepest gratitude goes to Dustin DiPerna of Bright Alliance Publishers for the personal touch he gave to the publication of this precious set of teachings, and Brad Reynolds, the type-setter, for his masterful layout and sensitive handling of these complex scriptures. Thanks also to Roger and Brenda Gibson, whose generous donation paid for the translation, and to the Pointing Out the Great Way Foundation for sponsoring these translation projects.

The Twenty-One Nails

Introduction

The *Twenty-One Nails* is the companion text to the *Six Lamps*. Both texts represent seminal transmission teachings of the Bon Great Completion (Dzogchen). The source of these teachings is said to be Tapihritsa, a very advanced Bon yogi who lived and practiced in the Mt. Kailash region of Tibet in the 7th century. He is said to have become an awareness-holder and lineage-holder who, after his complete enlightenment, had the ability to emanate in whatever form and whatever place he intended. According to the tradition, Tapihritsa foresaw that a great Bon *tantric* yogi, Gyer spungs sNang bzher Lod po, would be the kind of person worthy of receiving and teaching these precious transmission teachings to begin the Zhang Zhung Oral Transmission Lineage. However, sNang bzher Lod po was afflicted with considerable spiritual pride about his meditative experiences and realizations, so Tapihritsa was determined to cure him of that. Therefore, through his enlightened intention, Tapihritsa appeared in a temporary human form to sNang bzher Lod po, disguised as a 16 year-old boy. The boy showed up at sNang bzher Lod po's meditation hermitage and offered to serve him. He agreed to take on the boy as an apprentice. The two of them often talked about spiritual practice. The boy frequently asked very penetrating questions, and sNang bzher Lod po often found himself getting angry with the boy who frequently seemed to know more than he did. These angry episodes culminated in a flash of rage wherein sNang bzher Lod po challenged the boy to a public debate in front of the local king. The boy declined saying that such debate would only embarrass sNang bzher Lod po and expose him as being overly conceptual about spiritual practice. To emphasize his point, Tapihritsa walked right through the table. Immediately, sNang bzher Lod po realized that this was not an ordinary boy but a very great master. He humbled himself before Tapihritsa. Sat-isfied that sNang bzher Lod po had gone beyond his spiritual pride, Ta-pihritsa gave him the Bon Great Completion teachings in the form of two texts—the *Six Lamps* and the companion text, the *Twenty-One Nails*. These precious teachings constitute the origins of the extensive Zhang Zhung Oral Transmission Lineage of Bon Great Completion meditation.

BON GREAT COMPLETION LINEAGES

There are four Bon Great Completion lineages. The most extensive teachings come from the Zhang Zhung Oral Transmission Lineage attributed to Tapihritsa and sNang bzher Lod po. There are two systems of transmission in the Zhang Zhung Oral Transmission Lineage—the Four Cycles of Authoritative Transmission (*bka' rgyud skor bzhi*), and the Experiential Transmission (*nyams rgyud*). The second system is the *A Khrid* lineage, which is said to have originated with dGongs mdzod Ri khrod Chen po (1038-1096). We have already translated the well-known root text and auto-commentary of the ninth *A Khrid* lineage holder, Bru rGyal ba g.Yung drung (1242-1290).[1] The third system of Bon is sometimes referred to simply as Great Completion (*rdzogs chen*), but also as the Epit-ome Lineage (*yang rtse*). The fourth is the Removing Limits to the Primor-dial Throne Lineage (*ye khri mtha' sel*), attributed to Lung ston Lha gnyan in the 11th century.

THE CONTEXT OF BY-PASSING PRACTICE

Bon Great Completion has two main systems of practice: (1) thor-oughly cutting through (*khregs chod*) and (2) by-passing (*thod rgal*). Ac-cording to Shar rDza Rinpoche, the main difference between the two pertains to the degree of purification of the residuals or "dregs," (*snyig ma*) of the ordinary mind, and the relative degree to which the bright-ness (*dwangs ma*) of the awakened mind-itself shines forth free of these

---

1. Bru rGyal ba g.Yung drung, *Pith instructions for A Khrid rDzogs Chen*. Translated by Geshe Sonam Gurung and Daniel P. Brown. Occidental, CA: Bright Alliance for Point-ing Out the Great Way Foundation, 2017.

residuals. By-passing completely purifies these residuals whereas thoroughly cutting through does not. By-passing represents the complete exhaustion of any residuals of the ordinary mind pertaining to perception (like seeing mountains as solid), the visions, purifying the aggregates of the physical body (attaining rainbow body), eradicating subtle dualistic grasping, the fruition, namely serving the welfare of others, and the eternal ground of the path.

Both the *Six Lamps* and the *Twenty-One Nails* constitute very important, seminal by-passing Bon Great Completion practices. The *Six Lamps* is a main set of teachings and pith instructions on the levels of visions in by-passing practice. The *Twenty-One Nails* is an overview of twenty-one essential points on the view of ultimate reality in by-passing practice. The term "nail" (*gzer bu*) in Tibetan has a similar meaning to the word nail as it is used in colloquial English. When a professional gymnast does a perfect routine, we say that he or she "nailed" the routine. Similarly, when an advanced yogi or yogini penetrates the essential points of a set of pith instructions and comes to the full measure of realization, a Tibetan would say that the yogi or yogini "nailed" the realization. The text presents twenty-one essential points on the view of ultimate reality in by-passing meditation for the practitioner to "nail." Furthermore, there are two levels of "nailing" the essential points of a set of pith instructions. The first is nailing the essential points of what is directly pointed out. The second is nailing the realization at a more refined, intimate level of practice. This is called "making a close-to-the-heart determination" (*dmar thag chod*). The introduction to the commentary says that the essential points of the *Twenty-One Nails* pertain to making a close-to-the-heart determination for nailing or penetrating the secret of the natural state (568). Each of the twenty-one essential points is designed for "both intellectual understanding and direct realization [of the natural state]" (571)

A Brief Explanation of Each of the Twenty-One Nails

1: The Nail of Realizing the Universal Basis

The essential point begins with an introduction to the universal basis or groundless ground of existence (*kun gzhi*). The ground of existence is a limitless expanse or matrix within which everything arises. Yet, since it has no real substance to it, it is a groundless ground of being. The direct realization of the universal ground is the "embodiment of all the teachings," the literal meaning of the technical term *dharmakāya* (*bon sku*). For those who fail to recognize their true nature, the universal basis or groundless ground becomes the depository or reservoir for millions of habitual karmic propensities (*bag chags*), some of which become activated and ripen in such a way as to have influence over their outlook, behavior, and even determine the type of events encountered in everyday life. This overlay of habitual karmic memory traces in the ground changes the experience of the ground. Therefore, it is given the name storehouse consciousness (*kun gzhi rnam shes*) with respect to the ordinary person. Yet, ultimately, the groundless ground is never altered by nor affected by the activity of ripening habitual karmic memory traces within its domain.

As the commentary states, "The first nail refers to the realization of the universal base." (571) As the text says, these teachings are not for everyone. They are for those who have a previous karmic connection with the teachings, "who have become disheartened with *saṁsāra*," and who trust in their lama and these teachings. (572) Since these precious pith instructions are meant to be put into practice through intensive meditation, the root text says that the practitioner "should dwell in an isolated place in the mountain regions." (550) The main goal of meditation practice is to make a close-to-the-heart determination "to realize the difference between ordinary mind and awakened mind-itself" [and to realize] "the co-emergent universal ground [in] the full measure of its profundity." (572)

2: The Nail that Cuts Through Delusion to Primordial Purity

The second essential point is to cut through the misperception or delusion of the ordinary external world as well as internal conceptual thought, emotion, and the ripening of habitual karmic propensities. By making a close-to-the-heart determination about the delusion of the ordinary mind, according to the root text, "[they] realize the conditions [supporting] delusion, and have determined [the nature of] delusion." (551) By not making such a determination, the commentary adds, they will fail to realize the awakened mind-itself or the universal ground. The commentary says, "When they become deluded by any of their karma, they cannot realize the natural state and the universal ground." (577) The metaphor used to illustrate delusion is a lion looking at his reflection in a pool of water and failing to recognize it as his own form. (577)

Furthermore, once the practitioner has made an accurate determination about the delusion of the ordinary world, he or she directly perceives the pure visions: ordinary sound becomes the sound of lively awakened awareness expressing itself; visual forms, tastes, smells, and body sensation become the pure light of lively awakened awareness; and thought and emotions, because they have the property of directionality, become the liveliness of light-rays. Here the teachings introduce the by-passing visions. The different levels of vision are introduced through metaphors. At the first level, the visions come rapidly like a mountain waterfall. At the second level, the visions proliferate and fill the space "like arriving at a great river." (578) Eventually the moving energy drops slow down and become stationary. Each energy drop is like a computer chip that contains the same entire world of pure *Buddha* realms within it. At the third level, once they become stationary, the practitioner searches inside these energy drops and opens up the direct perception of the pure realms "like a bird of prey searching for food." (578) At the fourth level, the visions reach full measure, run their course, and wind down like a turtle in a basin that stops moving. (578) At the fifth or last level, the visions disappear or "exhaust" themselves (*zad pa*) "like the sky where the elements become exhausted into the universal ground." (578) Ultimately, the practitioner comes to realize that all these levels of visions are none other than the liveliness of awakened awareness, and the expression of enlightened intention, and "are [the manifestation of] *bodhicitta*." (578)

3: The Nail of the Expanse of *Dharmadhātu* Pervading Everywhere Impartially

When a practitioner sets up the view of the limitless expanse of aware-ness space, and through that goes beyond the localization of individual consciousness to recognize lucid, sacred awakened awareness as being always right here, the outcome of this realization is the *dharmakāya* (liter-ally, "the embodiment of all the teachings"). Once becoming more famil-iar with awakened mind-itself, the view naturally shifts from the ground aspect of awakening to the appearance aspect of awakening, in that the view now becomes viewing whatever arises in that expanse of limitless space as a continuous flow of the liveliness of awakened awareness. The technical term, *dharmadhātu*, is used to refer to the expanse within which this liveliness occurs, namely the matrix of the ground or expanse within which whatever occurs is lively awakened awareness within that matrix. The *dharmadhātu* is also the matrix within which the by-passing visions arise. As the commentary says, the expanse of *dharmadhātu* "abides every-where [in space] without edges or center, without cardinal or intermediate directions, without outside or inside, and without surface or depth... [and is] all-pervasive and all-encompassing." (578) This potential for events to arise as expressions of the liveliness of awakened awareness constitutes enlightened intention (*dgongs*) or *bodhicitta*. According to the commentary there are nine characteristics of *bodhicitta*: it arises without limits; it arises as infinite; it arises free of limitations; it arises without surface or depth; it arises immeasurably; it arises free of fear; it arises as a spectacular display; it arises inexhaustibly; and it arises without change. (578) This *dharma-dhātu* exists everywhere. As the commentary says, "This expanse abides within *Buddhas* and sentient beings alike." (578)

4: The Nail of Mind-Itself, Primordial Wisdom's Self-Awakened Awareness without Covering or Obscuration

The next essential point is the introduction of the five types of pri-mordial wisdom. The commentary says, "The ultimate truth of *bodhi-citta* stays as self-arising primordial wisdom." (579) Primordial wisdom manifests in five distinct ways. The commentary says, "[Primordial wis-dom] being empty and identityless... arises as what is called 'emptiness primordial wisdom.'" "[Perception] free of thought... arises as what is called 'mirror-like primordial wisdom.'" "[Thought] unadulterated and thoroughly complete... arises as what is called 'discriminating primordial wisdom.'" "Because it arises as undivided sameness, it arises as what is called 'sameness primordial wisdom.'" "Because it arises without effort as spontaneously present, it arises as what is called 'all-accomplishing primordial wisdom.'" (580) After introducing the five primordial wisdoms, the commentary reminds us that they are "the same, without [any real] distinctions." (580)

5: The Nail of What is Completely Pure from the Beginning, which is the Thumb-Sized *Dharmadhātu*

The next essential point introduces the heart lamp. In by-passing Great Completion meditation, the practitioner focuses on the area about the size of a quarter, or thumb-sized, as a space within the center of the physical heart. By holding the view continuously on this point of focus, while the view comes out of a back-drop of the limitless space of the universal ground, the localization of individual consciousness falls away and the practitioner directly realizes the bright lucidity of limitless awakened awareness. By sustaining focus on the heart lamp, the lucidity of awakened awareness gets brighter and brighter. The commentary says, "There arises naturally the thumb-sized great light that seems to appear... [and] you are never separated from [it]... [awakened awareness is] lucid and clear." (582) What arises at this thumb-sized focal point becomes limitless. As the root text continues, "It is called, 'the great appearance of the *dharmakāya*,'" literally, "the embodiment of all the teachings." (553) The commentary explains, "This thumb-sized light is referred to as a 'body' because it is unchanging." The metaphor of an enlightened body is meant to convey the absolute stability of *dharmakāya*. Just as a body has sense-organs, the metaphor continues that *dharmakāya* has divine eyes. The root text says, "These divine eyes are never covered by obscuration." (553) With this realization, everything is seen clearly for what it is. The text goes on to explain the significance of the *dharmakāya*, wherein everything that comes into existence is none other than the play of the liveliness of awakened awareness with the universal ground. As the commentary says, "It stays as the basis of everything that appears and as the root of all that arises, such as all that arises in *saṁsāra* and *nirvāṇa*, the eons, and the existing realms, etc." (585) As this universal ground is unconditioned, it cannot be affected by any causes and conditions. The essential point is that the direct realization of the limitlessness of awakened awareness makes a direct connection to the *dharmakāya* aspect of ultimate reality. The next essential points introduce the other two of the three-fold embodiment of enlightenment.

6: The Nail of Awakened Awareness-itself, which is the Completion Body [*Sambhogakāya*], i.e., Unification

Next, the text introduces the essential teachings on the pure realms of the *sambhogakāya* or completion body. The *sambhogakāya* does not refer to some remote reality that the practitioner travels to. The sacred realms of the *mandala* are always right here, yet ordinary individuals fail to perceive the sacredness of what surrounds them because their perception is impure and deluded. However, the by-passing practitioner gradually purifies ordinary perception so that they perceive the sacred *mandala* that is always right here. The essential point of this purification process is to hold the view of the inseparable pair—the limitless expanse, and the continuous liveliness of whatever arises within that expanse—and let everything run its own course without any mental engagement. Mental engagement creates new karmic memory traces. Holding the view of the inseparable pair, free of all mental engagement, sets up the continuous, automatic release of all ripening karmic memory traces, until the entire reservoir of karmic memory traces becomes exhausted. As a result, perception is purified and the practitioner no longer perceives an ordinary deluded world, but instead perceives the pure realms of the sacred mandala as always being right here. The commentary stresses that the view of the inseparable pair must be free of all residual duality. It says, "Universal ground and awakened awareness are without duality." (587) Once the purification process is brought to completion, all previous ordinary perceptions are transformed into the three by-passing visions—ultimate sound, light, and light-rays. The commentary adds, "These three visions are the root of everything [purified] in *saṁsāra* and *nirvāṇa*. Ultimate sound, light, and light-rays are the three great visions." (587) Additionally, all the pure realms of the *sambhogakāya* directly become manifest. The commentary continues, "All the visions of *nirvāṇa*—the celestial palaces, the pure realms, the *mandalas* and their ornaments, the colors of the bodies, the *mudras*, the major and minor marks, the principal deities, their retinues, and emanations, the five enlightened *Buddha* bodies, the five deity families, etc.—all these pure visions are complete as spontaneously present without effort [to produce them]." (587) All these spectacular visions constitute the "treasury" (588) of Great Completion practice. The root text says, "This is the treasury of the Great Completion wherein deities and their celestial palaces are unified." (555) The commentary explains, "With respect to the three visions, it is referred to as the 'celestial palace,' and all outer, inner, and secret *mandalas* arise from that." (588)

7: The Nail of Self-Awakened Awareness that is the Impartial Emanation Bodies [*Nirmāṇakāyas*]

The next teaching introduces the essential point of the third of the three-fold embodiment of enlightenment, namely the *nirmāṇakāyas*. The more stable the perception of the pure *Buddha* realms becomes, the stronger the aspiration develops within the heart of the practitioner on behalf of all those sentient beings in the six realms of *saṃsāra* that do not have this precious realization. The practitioner develops a sincere wish that all beings attain this realization and leave cyclic existence to become repopulated in awakened *dharmakāya* space. Eventually, the intensity of this aspiration explodes into immeasurable enlightened intentions in the form of emanations, each subduing the mind-stream of an individual sentient being and guiding him or her out of *saṃsāra* to enlightened *dharmakāya* space. The commentary refers to this display of immeasurable emanations or *nirmāṇakāyas* as "the magical display of *bodhicitta*." (591) Each emanation represents the enlightened intention to serve the welfare of sentient beings. These numerous emanations arise "impartially" and "without reference." (591) The entire world of cyclic existence co-emerges with the pure realms, and both *saṃsāra* and *nirvāṇa* become subsumed within a larger vision of ultimate realty, namely the single sphere of ultimate reality within which everything and everyone is interconnected by loving filaments of *bodhicitta* (*thig le chen po; nyag gcig*). The commentary says, "Everything is complete in the single sphere of ultimate reality of mind [wherein everything is interconnected]." (592)

8: The Nail that Eliminates the Darkness of Doubt Through Illustrative Examples

The next essential point pertains to the pith instructions that best point out the view of perception that dispels ordinary, deluded perception and fosters the realization of the sacred perception of visions in by-passing Great Completion meditation. These instructions are designed for the practitioner to make a "decisive determination" and to have "confidence" that such determination leads to mastery over ordinary, deluded perception. (593) Each of the illustrative examples—moonlight reflected on the surface of water, light-rays shining from the sun, light reflected from a crystal, and light shining from a butter lamp—is designed to show the "unified connection" between the seeming sense-object and awakened awareness, such that the seeming object is viewed as the manifestation of the liveliness of awakened awareness arising within the expanse of the universal ground. As the commentary says, "Awakened awareness is likened to the sun. The three visions are likened to light [rays from the sun]." (593)

Next, the teaching points out the same view over four conditions. According to the root text, "There are four occasions: staying [in the universal ground], the union [of body and mind at the beginning of life], the separation [of the mind from the body at death], and the delusion [that arises in the after-death states]." (556) First, if by-passing practice in this lifetime leads to the realization of the inseparable pair—the expanse and the continuous liveliness of whatever arises from within that expanse—the by-passing visions are likely to appear free of any obscuration. The commentary says, "Whenever there is staying in the universal ground and primordial awareness, awakened awareness is like the sun arising in a cloudless sky. The three—ultimate sound, light, and light-rays—stay without obscuration." (593-4) Second, if one hasn't practiced in this lifetime, ordinary perception is likely to be "obscured" and "deluded... like a butter lamp placed inside a pot," as the commentary says.

(594) Third, the dying process and the after-death *bardos*—when ordinary perception and conceptual thought completely drop away—become a unique opportunity to recognize the clear-light of death. Then, as the commentary says, "When the body and mind have become separated [at the time of death], this is when the after-death state of clear-light arises, and awakened awareness is like the sun in a cloudless sky. It arises clearly for the first time in this after-death state." (594) Fourth, during the *bardo* of rebirth, awakened awareness becomes "dull" and "arises like the sun covered by clouds, and awakened awareness becomes obscured by the appearance of delusion." (594) The objective of meditation practice is to use each of these four opportunities for "gaining mastery over the visions." (556) Ultimately, this pointing out teaching "show[s] ... the way of liberation" from which, according to the root text, "seeing this in-and-by-itself, and by means of this, the liberation of *Buddhahood* comes." (556) The essential point for liberation is to view the visions from a non-dual perspective and none other than lively awakened awareness arising within the expanse of the universal ground, and "not chase after these visions." (594) In other words, the essential point is to see the visions as "self-arising" (*rang shar*). (594) So that the practitioner not deviate from the correct view, the instructions remind the practitioner to search for an agent of these visions until it is unfindable and until it is clear that these visions self-arise without causes and conditions that make them arise. The commentary adds, "These just seem to occur from the liveliness of the natural state and, as such, have their own force. For example, it is like tongues of flame rising upward and like drops of water falling downward by their own force without an agent [making it happen]." (595) The root text concludes, "Make a determination about the heart-essence [of the mind] free of delusion, and there will be no more delusion." (556)

9: The Nail of the Depths of Self-Awakened Awareness Without Uniting With or Separating From It

The next essential point pertains to the stability of the realization of awakened awareness with heart lamp practice. Through making a close-to-the-heart determination, the practitioner comes to realize that awakened awareness is always right here in such a way that one neither unites with it nor separates from it. As the commentary says, "Since *bodhicitta* does not come from anywhere, it does not come from uniting to anything. Since it does not go anywhere, it cannot be separated from anything. This means that [*bodhicitta* is really] spontaneously present and co-emergent with the three times." Ordinarily, awakened awareness is "obscured" and special pith instructions are needed in order to realize it. As the commentary says, "Primordial wisdom's awakened awareness is said to be 'hidden' because it is difficult to realize, and said to be 'concealed' because it is [typically] covered by obscurations... like the stars that cannot be seen in the daytime." (596)

The physical heart lamp becomes the point of focus for the most likely realization of awakened awareness. As the commentary says, "Here, in the center of this offering tent... in the heart, primordial wisdom's awakened awareness is concealed much like placing a butter lamp in a [closed] pot... awakened awareness arises from within [this heart-space]... within the emptiness of the universal base." (597) The heart lamp is also the source of the visions, as seen through the eye lamps. The commentary continues, "The visions arise from the interior of this light [in the physical heart]." (597) The liveliness of awakened awareness within the heart lamp is like a "treasury of space" that is "the source of all phenomena of *saṃsāra* and *nirvāṇa* without exception." (597)

10: The Nail of the Self-Awakened Awareness that Uncovers the Straight Unmistaken Path

The next essential point makes a clear distinction between the "unmistaken path" based on the realization of primordial wisdom's self-awakened awareness, and the "deluded path" based on ordinary perception. The seemingly solid ordinary world arises when primordial wisdom is not recognized. The root text explains that the five wisdoms respectively evolve into the five wisdom lights, which evolve into the five pure elemental energies, which evolve into the five impure dregs, then the five elements, then the constituents of the physical body. Along this path of deluded perception, the physical body and the external world seem to become more substantial. This defines the pathway of *saṃsāra*. The unmistaken path is the pathway of the lamps or the pathway of *nir-*

vāṇa. This refers to the *kati* tube channel in by-passing practice that links the heart lamp to the fluid eye lamps through the upper central channel. As the commentary says, "This means that because this wind leaves the center of the heart and opens into the interior tube of the upper central channel, it arises in the gateway of the path to *nirvāṇa.* If awakened awareness is transferred from the upper central channel [at the time of dying] you attain the fruition of *nirvāṇa.*" The root text adds, "The central [channel] is the path wherein *saṃsāra* and *nirvāṇa* become non-dual." (557) This upper central channel is where the light of the visions arises. (600) The commentary adds that this channel location is where "awakened awareness arises in an unconstructed manner, in its own way." (601)

The last instruction is on consciousness-transference. The reason that consciousness-transference is introduced here is that by-passing practice sets the foundation for consciousness-transference, irrespective of whether the practitioner previously did or did not do practices to widen the upper central channel. As the commentary says, "This means that it is not necessary to be taught by a master [regarding consciousness-transference]." (602) The commentary also says, "If you were to transfer consciousness from this channel, it would no longer be possible to be re-born in *saṃsāra*... Riding along the path of the central channel consciousness-transference occurs at the crown *chakra.*" (602) In this manner, the by-passing practitioner blocks the gateways to rebirth and the three-fold embodiment of enlightenment becomes manifest. (603)

11: The Nail of Dispelling the Delusion of Non-Awakened Awareness, the Lamp for Dispelling Darkness

The next essential point is an introduction to the fluid eye lamps used to purify visual perception in by-passing practice. The practitioner views the arising visions just below the boundary of the eyebrow fence at a distance of the outer surface of the eyes, seeing the visions arise on the outer surface of the fluid eye lamps, much like watching images appear in two crystal balls. There, the visions appear completely free of all conceptual thought and all mental constructions. The commentary says, "With respect to the five gateways of the sense faculties, the king of awakened awareness arises free of thought much like a clean mirror.

The play of the seeming five external sense-objects arises like reflections in a mirror. Even though they arise, the king of awakened awareness is free of even the smallest particle of conceptual thought grasping at an object." (604) In ordinary perception, the mind-consciousness utilizes conceptual thought to appraise and interpret sense experience. In by-passing practice, there is no conceptual thought such that there is direct, pure perception of sense experience. By viewing the visions in this manner, the root text says, "the thickened darkness of the seeming ordinary world of appearance becomes purified." (558) Furthermore, the root text adds, "the darkness of non-recognition of awakening is dispelled in-and-by-itself." (605) By viewing these self-arising visions, our ordinary perception is completely purified until all deluded perception becomes exhausted "like a lotus that arises from the mud." (558) Purified perception "arises naked and bare, without being stained by anything whatsoever." (606) Purified perception is likened to seeing with "divine eyes." The commentary says, "In this way, in the gateways of the eye lamps the six divine eyes arise continuously in-and-by-themselves, and if the realization of each of these is bare and naked, then the ultimate truth of the natural state and the enlightened intentions of *Buddhahood* are completed, without remainder." (606)

12: The Nail of Beyond Being United With or Separated From the Three-fold Embodiment of Enlightenment, Pointing Out the Three Essential Points

The next essential point pertains to the stability of the three-fold embodiment of enlightenment. If ultimate reality is always right here as spontaneously present, then the practitioner goes beyond episodes of uniting with it, or losing it. The text introduces each of the three enlightened bodies. The essential point of introducing the *dharmakāya* is the experience of it as "limitless." (607) The essential point of the *sambhogakāya* is complete purification of ordinary perception and conceptual interpretation of ordinary perception, such that the pure *Buddha* realms are directly perceived as always right here. The essential point of the *nirmāṇakāyas* is the strength of the aspiration that develops to guide others along the path out of *saṃsāra* through strengthening enlightened intention so much that it explodes into immeasurable emanations, each serving the purpose of different sentient beings.

Next, there are instructions for the gradual development of the three-fold embodiment of enlightenment. Basis enlightenment refers to the initial experience of the three-fold embodiment of enlightenment. However, this initial experience is not typically very stable and is easily lost. Path enlightenment refers to the gradual development of the direct manifestation of the three enlightened bodies. Through the experience of the limitlessness of the expanse, *dharmakāya* usually becomes stable first. Through the gradual purification process, stable perception of the pure *Buddha* realms of the *sambhogakāya* gradually replaces the deluded perception of the ordinary external world. As the practitioner only perceives the pure realms, the aspiration develops for all those who fail to perceive these sacred realms to attain them, and through the maturation of this enlightened intention the emanations of the *nirmāṇakāyas* gradually develop. At some point all three enlightened bodies manifest in a stable manner. This is the endpoint, fruition enlightenment, and the practitioner goes beyond episodes of either uniting with it or losing it ever again. As the commentary explains, "This is the path to *Buddhahood* without going astray." (608)

In by-passing practice, the three enlightened bodies arise in three of the lamps, respectively. As the root text says, "The self-awakened awareness that arises from within the domain of the physical heart is the *dharmakāya*. In the path of the [*kati*] channel, its real nature is the *sambhogakāya*. In the gateways of the [fluid eye] lamps are the self-arising *nirmāṇakāyas*." (559)

13: The Nail of Self-Awakened Awareness, the Root Deity, Pointing Out the *Mandala*

The next set of instructions point out the essential features of the *mandala* of the pure *Buddha* realms. The commentary says that it is not necessary to visualize the features of the *mandala* because in by-passing practice they are already spontaneously present. The commentary says, "With respect to *bodhicitta*, it is not necessary to visualize the *mandalas* of the deities of *Mahamudrā* because they are explained as being complete in their own way." (610) The commentary continues: "The five kinds of [wisdom] lights are explained as the basis of arising of the pure realms of the Completion Body and the Emanation Bodies.... The energy drops of the offering tent of the five lights and the energy drops of awakened awareness that are crystal-like are explained to be the basis of arising of the celestial palaces of the five *Buddha* families.... The *mandalas* of the deities of *Mahamudrā* arise in the mind, but are not brought about through any effort as in the lower vehicles. This great *mandala* by nature arises as spontaneously present." (611)

14: The Nail of the Enlightened Body that is the Self-Occurring Single Interconnected Sphere

Once the manifestation of enlightenment becomes stable and reaches full measure, the single great sphere of ultimate reality becomes manifest within which everything and everyone is interconnected by loving filaments of *bodhicitta*. The commentary explains, "The inherent radiance of *bodhicitta* arises thoroughly pervading and encompassing all of seeming existence." (612) The root text adds, "The full measure of the visions is the play of the enlightened body. The full measure of speech is the play of enlightened speech. The full measure of mind is the play of the enlightened heart-mind. The full measure of the elements is the play of the [enlightened] positive qualities. The full measure of doing is the play of enlightened activity." (560) In other words, in addition to the manifestation of the three-fold embodiment of enlightenment, the full array of positive qualities flourish, and along with that comes inexhaustible enlightened activity toward all sentient beings. According to the commentary, by-passing practice has reached completion. "This means that within awakened mind-itself, within this single, interconnected sphere, nothing is not complete in all the phenomena of *saṁsāra* and *nirvāṇa*, and thus, everything is completed as the same taste in this [awakened] mind." (613)

15: The Nail of Being Without the Obscuration of Karmic Propensities, Making the Determination of Mother and Son

The next explanation pertains to the nature of purification. Purification entails allowing whatever arises as lively awakened awareness
within the expanse of *dharmadhātu* to run its own course without mental
engagement, and, as a result, all karmic memory traces that arise are immediately liberated, leaving no trace. The commentary says, "*Bodhicitta*
is completely pure without any kind of [karmic] attachments.... However, because of taking up the practice of this path, there is liberation from
the direct manifestation of these [karmic propensities] afflictive emotions... [and] the [overall] effect thereafter is that afflictive emotions can
never again develop." (613-14) As a result of this thorough purification,
bodhicitta is completely purified and is therefore experienced as all-pervasive, empty and clear; becomes free of all doing; is free of all expressions;
is free of all conceptualization; remains as self-occurring primordial wisdom; and serves as the basis of arising of all the by-passing visions. (615)
Furthermore, all of these—the elements of the existing world, various
actions, various expressions, all kinds of conceptual thought, the afflictive emotions, and the pure by-passing visions—are all manifestations of
the liveliness of awakened awareness. However, making any of these too
real and chasing after them leads back to the pathway of delusion. On
the other hand, completing the purification process defines the pathway
out of cyclic existence. As the commentary says, "If one cuts to the roots
like this, and [specifically] cuts to the roots of habitual karmic propensities, it is no longer possible to become re-born in any place in *saṁsāra.*"
(616)

16: The Nail of Non-Localization, Going Beyond, Crossing Over

The next essential point is designed to correct residual impurities
regarding the view used to cross over from ordinary mind to awakened
mind-itself. First, the view must be limitless and non-localized. The commentary says, "Because *bodhicitta* does not abide anywhere in any limits
throughout *saṁsāra* and *nirvāṇa*, it is said to go beyond everything as *nirvāṇa.*" (616) This view furthermore must be beyond all partial or extreme
views like eternalism or nihilism, (617) beyond all conceptualization
about it, beyond all attachment to or aversion to the pure visions, beyond

all categorization, beyond all duality, and beyond schools of thought and paths. The root text says, "Everything remains as sameness, without [distinctions like] good or bad, higher or lower." (562)

17: The Nail of Reaching the Endpoint, Being Victorious in the Embodiment of Enlightenment

The next essential point defines the endpoint of the by-passing path as *dharmadhātu* exhaustion of all the visions, ending in the stable manifestation of the three-fold embodiment of enlightenment. Here the visions reach "full measure." (619) The commentary says, "All the elements and all of the [forms of the] seemingly existing world, as much as it is, reach an end in the great emptiness/clarity of space." (619) Likewise, the commentary adds, "The ordinary mind and all the mental content, as much as there is, reach an end." (619) In other words, all conceptual thought and afflictive emotions become exhausted in the expanse. Furthermore, "All the paths, which are constructed by conceptual thought, such as the views, meditations, etc., reach an end." (619) Specifically, with respect to by-passing practice, all visions come to an end or become exhausted. The commentary says, "All the visions of ultimate sound, light, and light-rays reach an end in primordial wisdom's self-arising awakened awareness." (620) In sum, "everything without exception in *saṁsāra* and *nirvāṇa* is exhausted as *bodhicitta*." (620) Moreover, by-passing practice has become so strong that everything becomes liberated "at [the very point of just beginning to] occur," and in so doing becomes completely exhausted. (562) While the visions become exhausted, the perceptions of the ordinary world as appearing to others nevertheless arise in an unobstructed manner as "the magical display of *bodhicitta*." (620)

18: The Nail of Compassion that Protects Beings From the Jaws of Death

This teaching pertains to the essential pith instructions for utilizing the dying process and after-death *bardos* for realization. There are three sets of instructions according to best, middling, and lesser capacity practitioners. According to the commentary, at the time of death, "[the individual] is propelled by the [karmic] strength of good or bad thoughts, and there is a significant difference [in the direction taken]." Therefore, it is very important to have a [solid] foundation in the instructions. (621) Those of best capacity are taught to recognize awakened awareness during this lifetime so that during the dying process they are more likely to recognize the clear-light of death, and thereby attain liberation. Those of middling capacity are taught to recognize the by-passing visions as self-arising illusions, so that during the *bardo* of the *dharma-dhātu* they will come to see the similar visions as self-arising illusions, and thereby "close the gateways to [future] rebirths." (563) Those of lesser capacity are taught to remember the instructions about dying given by their root lama or tutelary deity (*yi dam*), and thereby will attain a favorable rebirth in their next life. In sum, what the practitioner has learned in by-passing meditation is relevant and applicable while dying and in the after-death states.

19: The Nail of Complete Self-Liberation and Buddhahood During the After-Death State

This section gives more detailed instructions on reaching *Buddhahood* during the after-death *bardos*. During the dying process, the physical elements, sense-objects, and all conceptual thought dissolve into the universal ground. (622) Those of best capacity use this dying process as a way to manifest enlightened body, speech, and mind, and reach complete *Buddhahood*. Those of middling capacity who do not reach liberation nevertheless stay in the natural state as they enter the *bardo* of *dharmadhātu* where the visions arise in the after-death state. They then use these after-death visions as a means to liberation. As the root text says, "For those individuals who are familiar with or acquainted with this, the enlightened bodies and the [entire array of the] *mandala* arise as complete." (564) For such practitioners, these pure *Buddha* realms are like an "old friend." By letting these visions arise unobstructedly, without mental engagement, the visions become completely purified and the residuals of ordinary experience, duality, and the physical body dissolve "like ice melting in an ocean," (564) and what remains is the pure, stable perception of the *Buddha* realms of the *mandala*, and they realize *Buddhahood*. Those of lesser capacity have only "slight familiarity" with the by-passing visions, and for them awakened awareness is likely to remain "dormant" in the after-death states, and the visions arise in an incomplete way. (564) Nevertheless, such practitioners can insure a favorable rebirth in their next life if they remember the instructions from their root lama during the dying process. Those individuals who have failed to enter the gateway of by-passing practice see the after-death visions as "real appearances." The root text adds, "They fall into the trap of delusion and wander [continuously] in *saṁsāra*." (565)

20: The Nail that Eliminates the Extremes of Mistaken Ideas

This section pertains to the topic of to whom these teachings should and should not be given. They should not be given to students who are not "proper vessels" to receive these teachings, such as those who: "do not realize the natural state;" "grasp after a self;" persist in holding extreme views; see the visions as "untrue;" "become attached to the three visions... as real;" and who criticize the teacher or the teachings. (629-30) The commentary says, "If [these instructions] are taught to those without a proper vessel, there are many ways to go astray thereafter. Therefore, the seal of secrecy should be affixed to these instructions."

21: The Nail of Realizing the Three Enlightened Bodies Directly, the Fruition

This last section is on stable enlightenment, or the complete fruition. The commentary says, "Those who have practiced with these instructions, and through them have made a decisive determination about the ultimate truth, will attain the fruition." Fruition entails complete purification of obscuration and delusion, and all conceptual thought arising as liveliness. The commentary says, "It is no longer possible for awakened awareness to become deluded throughout the places of *saṁsāra*." All partial views become exhausted. Additionally, fully manifest *Buddhahood* is stable. The commentary says, "Because the immutable, eternal [ultimate reality] has arisen in your own mind, it can't be stopped by any kind of adverse conditions." (633-34)

THE TWENTY-ONE NAILS
ACCORDING TO THE ZHANG ZHUNG ORAL TRANSMISSION LINEAGE OF BON DZOGCHEN

ROOT TEXT BY
TAPIHRITSA

AUTO-COMMENTARY ATTRIBUTED TO
GYERPUNG NANGZHER LODPO

TRANSLATED UNDER THE GUIDANCE OF
HIS HOLINESS THE THIRTY-THIRD
MENRI TRIZIN

BY GESHE SONAM GURUNG AND DANIEL P. BROWN, PH.D.

FOR MUSTANG BON FOUNDATION

Reader's Note:

The root text is in **bold Franklin Gothic**.

The Commentary is in Baskerville.

(Page numbers for the commentary are in parentheses.)

The root text begins:

(550) Homage to the all-pervasive and all-encompassing compassion of Kun tu bZang po!

In order for fortunate ones to carry the [realization of universal] ground in their mind-stream hereafter, here is the profound vital essence of the unsurpassed oral transmission secret instructions for cutting to the root of the universal ground, the natural state. Moreover, these are taught as the epitome of all the gateways of Bon, the ultimate great vehicle. The sacred instructions extract the heart-essence of the lineage. They are the sacred pith instructions resembling eyes [to see]. They [represent] the enlightened intention of the heart-mind, [originally] conveyed [mind-to-mind] and [later through] the oral transmission in words. [After that] these instructions were written down in lotus-blue ink on white conch paper by [sNang bzher Lod po directly from Tapihritsa]. They [both] were emanations [of previous] masters, who taught it to those gShen disciples with fortunate karma. Later, it was transmitted in succession to such individuals in subsequent generations.

Here are the essential points of the twenty-one nails. May they hit the targets, which are the minds of those fortunate enough to receive them. *Samaya!*

The Commentary begins:
(568) Here is the commentary on the twenty-one nails from the oral transmission of the Zhang Zhung Great Completion.

Homage to Kun tu bZang po, in the state of bliss!

These are the teachings that bring the 84,000 Bon teachings to their final endpoint—the special instructions of the enlightened intention of the mind-to-mind transmission of the *Sugatas*, the oral lineage of the twenty-four masters, and the experiential transmission lineage of accomplished yogis. With respect to these instructions on the essential points of Great Completion, there are four parts to the explanation:

(1) The outer explanation of general view,

(2) The inner explanation of special instructions and their close-to-the-heart determination,

(3) The secret explanation of seeing awakened awareness nakedly,

(4) The very secret explanation regarding penetrating the natural state. Among the four, these teachings are those that penetrate the [fourth] very secret way, namely the teachings on the twenty-one nails, which pertain to penetrating the natural state. [The root text of each of the twenty-one nails] has three parts—the introduction, the main teaching, and a conclusion.

The text begins with an introductory section that includes an explanation of the homage, an explanation of the significance of the teachings, and an explanation of the special instructions of the transmission lineage.

THE EXPLANATION OF THE HOMAGE

The root text says, "Homage to the all-pervasive compassion of Kun tu bZang po!"

When using examples to illustrate, "*kun*" refers to everything that exists and appears; "*bzang*" refers to the great emptiness and lucidity like space; (569) "*tshul*" refers to the way that is the same everywhere, such that there are no distinctions like good/bad, great/small, high/low, increase/decrease, or near/far; "*khyab bdal*" refers to being all-pervasive and all-encompassing without an above or a below, without cardinal or ordinal directions, without edges or borders or a center, and without a surface or depth; "*thugs rje*" refers to the culmination as immeasurable compassion.

When referring to the meaning, "*kun*" refers to all seemingly existing phenomena as having the phenomenal characteristics; "*bzang*" refers to the way that everything becomes equalized without partiality as having phenomenal characteristics; "*khyab bdal*" refers to abiding in [the expanse] without center or edge and without any directions or intermediary directions; "*thugs rje*" refers to the culmination of immeasurable compassion.

When referring to the signs [of progress], "*kun*" refers to the life-force and breath of every sentient being; "*bzang*" refers to the mind-itself wherein there is self-occurring primordial wisdom; "*bzang tshul*" refers to the manner of acting with complete impartiality and equality toward all sentient beings; "*khyab bdal*" refers to its completely saturating the three realms impartially without cardinal or intermediate directions; and "*thugs rje*" refers to the culmination of immeasurable compassion.

The homage is in accordance with general [teachings].

THE EXPLANATION OF THE SIGNIFICANCE OF THE TEACHINGS

The explanation of the significance of the teachings follows. The root text says, "In order for fortunate ones to carry the [realization of the universal] ground in their mind-streams hereafter...." This refers to those fortunate ones who through these instructions have been able to cross over on this path, in that they have been able to directly proceed to the natural state and the universal ground. The root text continues, "Here is the profound vital essence of the unsurpassed oral transmission secret instructions." This refers to four kinds of explanations [mentioned above], and among these, it specifically refers to the hidden instructions pertaining to the teaching on how to penetrate the natural state. (570) The root text continues saying, "instructions for cutting to the root of the universal ground, the natural state." This means that through these instructions you directly come to the natural state, the universal ground. This refers to the teachings that cut to the root. The root text then says,

"Moreover, these are taught as the epitome of the gateway of Bon, the ultimate great vehicle." The *gateway of Bon* refers to the 84,000 teachings [of Bon]. *Ultimate* refers to the fact that there is no other gateway that can surpass this. *Vehicle* refers to the nine stages [of Bon] and also to the external, internal, and hidden teachings. *Epitome* refers to the fact that there isn't anything else beyond this. The root text continues, "The sacred instructions extract the heart-essence of the lineage." All the *tantras* are like the physical body. These instructions are like the heart [of the body]. All the oral readings are like milk. These instructions are like the essence of the milk [the butter]. The root text continues, "They are the sacred pith instructions resembling eyes [to see]." All the gateways of Bon, all the vehicles and lineages [of Bon] are like having an extra sense system. These instructions are instructions that are like having bright eyes inside the sense organs.

An Explanation of the Special Instructions of the Transmission Lineage

Regarding the explanation of the special instructions of the transmission lineage, the root text continues, "They [represent the] enlightened intention of the heart-mind, [originally] conveyed [mind-to-mind], and the oral transmission by words." This refers to the unbroken lineage of the nine masters, the contemplation of the *Sugatas* that were not spoken in words, but from their contemplation were transmitted in contemplation [from mind-to-mind]. The oral transmission refers to the twenty-four masters who transmitted their teachings through words. Having heard the words, this refers to an oral transmission. The root text continues, "These instructions were written down in lotus-blue ink on white conch paper by sNang bzher Lod po from Tapihritsa." The root text continues, "They [both] were emanations [of previous] masters who taught it to those gShen disciples with fortunate karma." This refers to Guru Tapihritsa (571) giving these instructions to sNang bzher Lod po. The root text continues, "and it was transmitted in succession to such individuals of subsequent generations." This passage refers to how the victorious forefathers divinely watched over their [spiritual] children and transmitted these teachings in unbroken succession to future generations. The root text continues, "Here are the essential points on the twenty-one nails." This passage refers to the enumeration of teachings [on the natural state]. "May they hit the target for those fortunate to receive them." This passage refers to the wish that [those who receive them] find both intellectual understanding and direct realization [of the natural state]. "*Samaya!*" refers to the command to seal these instructions to keep them hidden so they won't degenerate. This completes the commentary on the introduction.

Second, there is an explanation of the meaning of each of the twenty-one nails.

1: The Nail of Realizing the Universal Basis

Homage to Kun tu bZang po for directly showing awakened awareness-in-itself. Those individuals who fear death and re-birth [in *samsāra*] in the depths [of their hearts] should dwell in an isolated place in the mountain regions conducive to pleasant experiences. They will come to realize the universal ground and make a close-to-the-heart determination about awakened awareness. (551) The king of awakened awareness, which is co-emergent [with the universal ground] is profound and is a rare jewel that is difficult and subtle to realize. Thus, special means are taught for this realization. On this path, the special means is distinguishing between [ordinary] mind and [awakened] mind-itself. [Begin with] the essential points of the body [posture], then restraining the horse of the winds is like restraining a horse of the energy currents. Establish the gateways of the lamps [especially the eye lamps] in their own way. The pith instructions for distinguishing between ordinary mind and awakened mind-itself are as follows: There is no analysis of external [perceptions]. There is no examination of internal thought. Do not chase after what came previously or what might come subsequently. Demonstrating the full measure of the distinction between ordinary mind and awakened mind-itself occurs through dissolving the residual [obscurations] in the domain [of space, such that what remains] is the brightness [of awakened awareness] as clear-light. By removing the outer layer of conceptual thought, awakened awareness arises nakedly. By purifying the mass of clouds of conceptual thought, primordial wisdom is no longer covered by obscuration.

Realizing [the distinction between] ordinary mind and awakened mind-itself has four [features]: it is absent of conceptual thought; it becomes the universal ground; it is neutral; and it is [the source of all] potential occurrences in an unobstructed [manner]. Additionally, these four are [the features of] the universal ground and awakened mind-itself.

Yet, whatever arises as recollections and [ordinary] mindfulness is liberated in a relaxed [state]. If established this way, it becomes mixed [back into] the universal ground. This is how ordinary conceptual thought and mind [become liberated].

Make a close-to-the-heart determination [about the distinction between] ordinary mind and awakened mind-itself as follows: by means of the three kinds of restraints, you let go of bodily distraction. Also, by means of the three [kinds of ways of] relaxing [the mind's] conceptual thought, it is brought into its natural condition. By means of the three skillful means to set up, you recognize awakened awareness in its own place. By means of the three [ways] of not engaging, habitual karmic propensities are interrupted. By means of the three ropes [of mindfulness], you extend the degree of familiarity. By means of the three secret means, you protect the ultimate realization from ways of being spoiled. By means of the three visions, you purify the liveliness of awakened awareness. By means of the three liberations, you become decisively free of duality. By means of the three non-obscurations, you reach the full measure of the fruition. This completes the nail of realizing the universal ground. *Samaya!* (552)

(571) The first nail refers to the realization of the universal base. There are three parts—the homage, the extensive explanation, and the conclusion.

First, there is an explanation of the homage. The root text says,

"Homage to Kun tu bZang po for directly showing awakened aware-ness-in-itself." "*Kun*" refers to subduing all beings without exception. "*bZang po*" refers to compassion that is never diminished, unceasing, and has complete equality [toward everyone]. *Directly showing awakened awareness in-and-by-itself* refers to these teachings, which show how to draw forth the natural state of awakened awareness nakedly. *Homage* refers to being in harmony with the general meaning [of the teachings].

Second, the extensive explanation has four parts: (1) Explaining which individuals should practice; (2) Explaining the place to practice; (3) Explaining the meaning of what is difficult to realize; and (4) Explaining the special instructions to distinguish between ordinary mind and awakened mind-itself.

First, Explaining Which Individuals Should Practice

The root text begins, "Those individuals who fear death and re-birth [in *saṃsāra*] in the depths [of their hearts]..." This pertains to such individuals on the path (572) who have become disheartened with *saṃsāra*. Having become fearful in their depths of death and re-birth, they seek to attain enlightenment. With inexhaustible trust they carry their lamas on the crowns of their heads, and from this moment on they give up all thought in the mind and seek the truth thereafter. This is the way they take up the practice of meditation.

Second, Explaining the Place to Practice

The teachings on the place are as follows: The root text continues, saying, [practitioners] "should dwell in an isolated place in the moun-tain regions conducive to pleasant experiences." This refers to remaining in an isolated place free from distractions and everyday busyness. They take up the practice in a place conducive to pleasant experiences coming to mind, such as an island or a forest, and there they practice over an extended period of time. The root text continues, "They will come to realize the universal ground and make a close-to-the-heart determina-tion about awakened awareness." This refers to recognizing [awakened awareness], making a determination about it, and developing confidence about it.

Third, Explaining the Meaning of What is Difficult to Realize

Explaining what is difficult to realize is as follows: The root text says, "The king of awakened awareness, which is co-emergent [with the universal ground], is profound and is a rare jewel that is difficult and subtle to realize." With respect to co-emergent universal ground, the full measure of its profoundness is like the depths of the ocean, or like the domain of [limitless] space. With respect to its subtlety, it is like the subtlety of the smallest of particles. Because of that, these instructions teach how to realize the difference between ordinary mind and awakened mind-itself.

Fourth, Explaining the Special Instructions to Distinguish Between Ordinary Mind and Awakened Mind-Itself

This section has five parts:

(1) The path of skillful means for distinguishing between ordinary mind and awakened mind-itself,

(2) The special instructions,

(3) Explaining the culmination of distinguishing them,

(4) Realizing [the difference between] ordinary mind and awakened mind-itself, and

(5) Making a close-to-the-heart determination.

First, the path of skillful means has three parts. Restraining the essential points of the body is as follows: Use the *mudras* that represent the inherent nature of the mind. By means of the body, the energy channels are controlled. By means of the energy channels, conceptual thought is controlled. (573) By means of the energy currents, the mind is controlled. By these, the natural lucidity of the universal ground is realized. The root text continues, "Restraining the winds is like restraining a horse of the energy currents." This means that the energy currents are like the horse and the sense-mind is like the person who rides the horse. Because of the movement of the six sense systems toward sense-objects, the universal ground is like the mother [consciousness] that becomes obscured. That is why it is called "restraining the horse of the energy currents." By restraining the horse of the energy currents, the sense-mind stops. By it stopping, the essence of the mother [consciousness] of universal ground becomes lucid. The root text continues, "Establish the gateways of the lamps in their own way." This means that without shutting the eyes, establish alert awakeness toward sense-objects. Through this gateway of seeing awakened awareness you come to realize the universal ground without conceptual thought.

Second, the passage in the root text called "the pith instructions for distinguishing between ordinary mind and awakened mind-itself" has three parts. Externally, because there is no analysis, one purifies [the duality] of grasper and grasped toward sense-objects. Internally, because one does not conceptualize about what is inside, one calms the mind's conceptual thought. Because one does not chase after anything before or after, one makes a decisive determination about the connection to the sense-mind.

Third, the passage called "demonstrating the full measure of distinguishing between ordinary mind and awakened mind-itself" has three parts. As mentioned previously there are three skillful means on the path and three pith instructions. By penetrating [the meaning] of these essential points, all the various residual recollections and conceptual thoughts are absorbed within the domain of the universal ground, and what becomes clear is self-occurring primordial wisdom as radiant light. For example, it is like water [settling down] free from being stirred up. Free from the outer layer of duality, primordial wisdom's awakened awareness arises nakedly, like a naked person not covered with any clothing. Through purifying the clouds of conceptual thought, non-conceptual primordial wisdom arises without any covering of obscurations, much like a cloudless sky.

Fourth, (574) realizing awakened mind-itself has two parts—realizing awakened mind-itself and realizing ordinary mind.

First, awakened mind-itself, the essence of the universal ground is non-conceptual. Yet, all the recollections and ordinary awareness that arise come from this universal ground. Whatever [conceptual thought] arises, but is neutral, has no limitations. Because whatever [conceptual thought] occurs is unobstructed, it is possible for it to arise in any way. These four are the essence of the universal ground, and one realizes this to be the existence of awakened mind-itself.

Second, realizing ordinary mind is as follows: Its essence is ordinary recollection and ordinary awareness. When one reflects, ordinary recollections and ordinary awareness can arise in any way. If one does not reflect and lets thoughts settle into their own way, they become liberated in-and-by-themselves in the state of the universal ground. If set up in an unconstructed way in that state, mother and son consciousness become inseparable. These four are referred to as "conceptual mind." It is also referred to as [concepts relevant to the] "sense-mind."

Fifth, the root text says, "Make a close-to-the-heart determination [about the distinction between] ordinary mind and awakened mind-itself." There are three sets of three essential points of the pith instructions, or nine essential points in all.

The root text continues, "By means of the three kinds of restraints you let go of bodily distraction." This refers to restraint of bodily activities, restraint of speech, and restraint of reflections and considerations of mind. Through these three [restraints] you let go of distraction.

The root text continues, "Also, by means of the three [kinds of ways of] relaxing [the mind's] conceptual thought, it is brought into its natural condition." This refers to relaxing bodily activity, relaxing speech, and relaxing the mind so it is without reflection. Through these three [kinds of ways of relaxing], conceptual thought is brought into its natural state. The root text continues, "By means of the three skillful means to set up, you recognize awakened awareness in its own place." This means that with respect to the ordinary mind everything is established in its own way without fabricated activity, everything is established in the greatness of its own manner, naturally, unadulterated and unfabricated. By these three [means] you end with awakened awareness in its own place. (575)

The root text continues, "By means of the three [ways] of not engaging, habitual karmic propensities are interrupted." There is no chasing after activities of the body. There is no chasing after spoken words. There is no chasing after the sensory pleasures of the mind. Through these three [ways of not chasing after], you interrupt habitual karmic propensities, which are based on chasing after.

The root text continues, "By means of the three ropes [of mindfulness] you extend the degree of familiarity." This refers to extending undistracted mindfulness, extending the duration of the state, without constructions, and extending the natural condition without disturbance. By these three [kinds of extensions] you extend the duration of the state without change in the domain of the universal ground.

The root text continues, "By means of the three secret means you protect the ultimate realization from ways of being spoiled." This refers to it being hidden in the body, like a wounded animal hiding, or like a butter lamp placed inside a pot. Even the smallest inclination toward speech remains without words. It is kept secret from others, and hidden in complete secrecy within oneself. Like a turtle inside the ocean, without chasing after the six senses, it is hidden in the mind, in the domain of the universal ground. By means of these three [secret means], nothing changes in the domain of the universal ground, and indestructible ultimate truth arises.

The root text continues, "By means of the three visions you purify the liveliness of awakened awareness." The various activities of the body arise as the liveliness of no activity. The various activities of speech arise as the liveliness of speechlessness. The various recollections of mind arise as the liveliness of no conceptual thought. Through these three you do not view the various [activities] as faults and they become purified as the liveliness of primordial wisdom.

The root text continues, "By means of the three liberations, you become decisively free of duality." The culmination of activity is being liberated in the domain that is without activity. The culmination of speech is liberated in the domain that is speechless. The culmination of reflection is liberated in the domain that is without reflection. (576) Through these three liberations, the [distinction] between ordinary mind and awakened mind-itself is gone.

The root text continues, "By means of the three non-obscurations, you reach the full measure of the fruition." Through the various activities of the body, nothing obscures the truth of being without activity. Through the various activities of speech, nothing obscures the truth of speechlessness. Through the various activities of mind, nothing obscures the truth of freedom from reflection. Through reaching the full measure of these, fruition directly becomes manifest.

Third, is the conclusion. The root text says, "This completes the nail of realizing the universal ground." This refers to the conclusion. The commentary on the first nail is now complete.

2: The Nail that Cuts Through Delusion to Primordial Purity

Homage to Kun tu bZang po, who is primordially purified of all delusion. Those fortunate ones who have given up the activities of the ordinary world, in the best place, free of [all] external distractions, realize the conditions [supporting] delusion, and have determined [the nature of] delusion. Beyond any doubt, they have subdued the sense-mind [such that liveliness as] ultimate sound, mental events [as] light, and thought [as] light-rays are [all] liveliness in the expanse [of the universal ground].

Take the middle count of the pulse of the channels, the one that is neither too fast nor too slow, and count this pulse continuously. With respect to one hundred beats, count them as a single beat. By [the time of reaching] 180,000 [of such beats], the familiarity with the four [levels of] visions reaches full measure and comes to an end. The light-rays of awakened awareness and the filaments of compassion are as follows: first, it is like water falling from a steep mountain; second, it is like arriving at a great river; third, it is like a bird of prey searching for food; fourth, it is like a turtle contained in a basin; and fifth, it is like the sky where the elements become exhausted into the universal ground. This completes the nail of cutting to the root of delusion. *Samaya!*

Second, is the nail that cuts to the root of delusion. The three sections include the homage, extensive explanation, and conclusion.

First, the homage is, "Homage to Kun tu bZang po, who is primordially purified of all delusion." "*Kun*" refers to everything in *saṃsāra* and *nirvāṇa* with nothing excluded. "*bZang*" refers to being thoroughly saturated by the impartial king of awakened awareness that knows itself-by-itself. "*Khrul pa ka nas dag*" [delusion as primordial purity] is like the heart of the sun that never remains in darkness. The king of knowing, awakened awareness is primordially pure and never remains in delusion. This is primordial purity. These instructions cut to the root of delusion, and through them you learn that delusion cannot exist.

Second, the extensive explanation is as follows: The root text says, "Those fortunate ones who have given up the activities of the ordinary world…" This refers to individuals who have taken up this meditation practice. The text continues, "in the best place free of [all] external distractions…" This passage refers to the [ideal] place for meditation practice. (577) The root text continues, "[they] realize the conditions [supporting] delusion, and have determined [the nature of] delusion." This briefly summarizes how to cut to the root of delusion. When they become deluded by any of their karma, they cannot realize the natural state and the universal ground. This is delusion. If they act according to the conditions [that support delusion] since they have made the conditions that support delusion by means of the three—ultimate sound, light, and light-rays—there is delusion. If they become deluded in that way, they will not know these three [visions] as self-appearing, and become deluded by seeing them as [real] external appearances.

What is an example of becoming deluded? It is like a reflection of a great lion arising in the water. The lion fails to realize that it is his own form, and sees it as the reflection of something else. Therefore, he is deluded. However, if you cut off becoming deluded in that way, through realizing the three—ultimate sound, light, and light-rays—as self-appearing, and then having made a decisive determination about delusion, delusion cannot exist. For example, with respect to one's own reflection, one knows it as one's own reflection. It is like meeting with an old friend you have known previously. If you come to realize this just as it is, you subdue the sense-mind with respect to ultimate sound, mental events with respect to light, and [thought] with respect to light-rays, and all are purified as liveliness. Make a determination regarding these three in the expanse of the universal ground. The way this is pointed out is known through the pith instructions.

The root text continues, "Take the middle count of the pulse of the channels, the one that is neither too fast nor too slow, and count this pulse continuously. With respect to one hundred beats, count them as a single beat. By [the time of reaching] 180,000 [such beats], the familiarity with the four [levels of] visions reaches full measure and comes to an end." These four passages show the full measure of the practice, and so they are elucidated as follows.

The root text continues, "The light-rays of awakened awareness and the filaments of compassion are as follows: first, [increasing visions] it is like water falling from a steep mountain." This means that at the time the visions first start to increase, the visions will roam about and not stay put even for a moment (578). Second, [proliferating visions] "is like arriving at a great river." This refers to the time when the visions start to proliferate. The visions are slower and more gentle than before. Rays and single filaments appear in a way like someone on foot, at first more rapidly, then more slowly. Third, [multiplying visions], as the root text continues, "is like a bird of prey searching for food." This refers to when the visions start to multiply. There are filaments of compassion, the heart-essence of awakened awareness. Sometimes they remain stable without wavering, and sometimes they move. Fourth [the completion of the visions] "is like a turtle contained in a basin." This refers to the time the visions come to completion. These filaments of compassion remain stationary, without wavering. Fifth [reaching the end], is described in the root text: "It is like the sky where the elements become exhausted into the universal ground." This refers to the time when the visions reach the endpoint. One makes the close-to-the-heart determination that the three visions—ultimate sound, light, and light-rays—are [the manifestation of] *bodhicitta*.

Third is the conclusion, which is clearly explained in the root text when it says, "This completes the commentary on the second nail."

3: The Nail of the Expanse of *Dharmadhātu* Pervading Everywhere Impartially

Homage to Kun tu bZang po, who is [the expanse] pervading everywhere without one-sidedness or partiality. The universal ground that arises universally is all-pervasive and all-encompassing. If we were to affix a name, this would be called "the expanse of *dharmadhātu*." Whatever arises has the nine characteristics of this expanse. Yet, like indivisible space, the entire display is the great sameness. This completes the nail of the expanse of *dharmadhātu*. Samaya! (553)

Third, is the nail of the expanse of the *dharmadhātu*. This is described in three sections [as before], the first [being the homage]. The root text begins, "Homage to Kun tu bZang po, who is [the expanse] pervading everywhere impartially." This passage explains the homage. "*Kun tu bZang po*" is explained in the same way as before. "*khyab dbal phyogs ris med pa* [pervading everywhere impartially]" refers to how *bodhicitta* abides everywhere [in space] without edges or center, without cardinal or intermediate directions, without outside or inside, and without surface or depth.

Second, is the extensive explanation. The root text says, "The universal ground that arises universally is all-pervasive and all-encompassing." This passage describes how *bodhicitta* is the universal ground of everything, [containing all] *Buddhas* and sentient beings throughout *saṁsāra* and *nirvāṇa*. The root text continues, "If we were to affix a name, this would be called 'the expanse of the *dharmadhātu*.'" Why is it called this? The root text answers, "Whatever arises has the nine manifestations of this expanse." [These nine characteristics are]: *bodhicitta* arises without limits; it arises as infinite; it arises completely without limitations; it arises without surface or depth; it arises immeasurably; it arises without fear; it arises as the spectacular display; it arises inexhaustibly; and it arises without change. Therefore, it is called "expanse." As an example of this, the root text says, "Yet, like indivisible space, the entire display is the great sameness." This means that this expanse abides within *Buddhas* and sentient beings alike without distinctions like good/bad, great/small, top/

bottom, increasing/decreasing, or near/far, etc.

Third the conclusion is clearly expressed in the root text when it says, "This completes the commentary on the third nail."

4: The Nail of Mind-Itself, Primordial Wisdom's Self-Awakened Awareness without Covering or Obscuration

Homage to Kun tu bZang po's self-awakened awareness without covering or obscuration. This [awakened awareness] is co-emergent and arises by itself within the universal ground. This is called "awakened mind-itself, primordial wisdom's awakened awareness." Through the five essential characteristics of primordial wisdom having arisen, they [each] seem distinct and unmixed, like [individual] rays of the sun, yet they remain as the same evenness [everywhere]. This completes the nail of awakened mind-itself, primordial wisdom. *Samaya!*

Fourth is the nail of primordial wisdom's awakened mind-itself. This section has three parts. The first is the homage. The root text begins, "Homage to Kun tu bZang po's self-awakened awareness, without covering or obscuration." This passage explains the homage. This means that the ultimate truth of *bodhicitta* stays as self-arising primordial wisdom.

Second is the extensive explanation. The root text says, "This [awakened awareness] is co-emergent, and arises by itself within the universal ground." This means that light-rays of primordial wisdom's awakened awareness are found within the mind-stream of each and every *Buddha* and sentient being alike. If we were to affix a name to this it would be called "awakened mind-itself, primordial wisdom's awakened awareness," as described in the root text. (580) Why is it called this? The root text says, "Through the five essential characteristics of primordial wisdom having arisen." This passage refers to [primordial wisdom] being empty and identityless, and therefore, it arises as what is called "emptiness primordial wisdom." With respect to this lucidity, since it is free of thought, these arise as what is called "mirror-like primordial wisdom." Because it is unadulterated and thoroughly complete, it arises as what is called "discriminating primordial wisdom." Because it arises as undivided sameness, it arises as what is called "sameness primordial wisdom." Because it arises without effort as spontaneously present, it arises as what is called "all-accomplishing primordial wisdom." Hereafter these will be referred to as "[the five essential characteristics of] primordial wisdom." If you were to ask for an example of what this is like, the root text says, "It is like [individual rays of] the sun, yet they remain as the same evenness [everywhere]." This means that each of these [distinct primordial wisdoms] arises in the mind-stream of each and every individual, and yet they stay the same, without [any real] distinctions such as good/bad, great/small, etc.

Third, the conclusion is clearly expressed in the root text when it says, "This completes" the commentary on the fourth nail.

5: The Nail of What is Completely Pure from the Beginning, which is the Thumb-Sized *Dharmakāya*

Homage to Kun tu bZang po's self-awakened awareness that is primordially pure. The king of self-occurring awakened awareness is lucid, such that self-occurring primordial wisdom stays at its root in the universal ground. This formless primordial wisdom is devoid of color, shape, or form. This inexpressible primordial wisdom is devoid of names, words, or letters. This thought-free primordial wisdom is [devoid of] thought, analysis, or ideas. This thumb-sized primordial wisdom [that abides in the heart] and has no [substantial] appearance is the *dharmakāya*. This is referred to as gShen lha dKar po [The Purest Bon deity], but has no real designation as the universal ground. Among its numerous names it is also called "awakened awareness that is the essence-itself."

From this thumb-sized great primordial wisdom and its lucidity, there arises naturally the thumb-sized great light that seems to appear. This light arises in-and-by-itself in such a way that you are never separated from it or need to become integrated with it. With respect to its lucidity, this [light] appears as insubstantial and without inherent nature. It is without form or color, and without any partiality. It is beyond a measure of any size, like large or small, and any measure of weight. It is called "the great appearance of the *dharmakāya*." It is also called the root deity who is given the designation gShen lha dKar po [The Purest Bon deity]. Among its numerous names it is called "the awakened awareness that appears through special insight."

Whenever the divine eyes of primordial wisdom arise with respect to this thumb-sized *dharmakāya*, it completely sees everywhere in all ten directions, but its enlightened body has neither front nor back. Without looking it sees everywhere. (554) These divine eyes are never covered by obscuration. Everything arises as this great transparency without outside or inside and remains as all-pervasiveness without edge or center. It remains all-pervasive and all-encompassing, and arises in the [expanse of the] universal ground, unstained by anything whatsoever. Primordially staying, it [nevertheless] arises as the play of the previously mentioned king of awakened awareness. Here [in this primordial condition] there is no *samsāra* or *nirvāna*, no cycles of time—just the occurrence of the king of awakened awareness in the primordial ground. Here, [primordially] there is no accomplishment of *Buddhahood*, nor any mandate to become a *Buddha*. Here there is no becoming an ordinary sentient being because individuals were not created from their [karmic] efforts. Here there are no causes and conditions because its real [primordial] nature remains unconditioned. The container [this world as we know it] did not originate from even the smallest particle. Here the physical body was not created from causes, namely the [five] elements. Here it did not come from [the father's] semen or the mother's womb. Here there is no cause for either realization of *nirvāna* or delusion of *samsāra*. Here, this self-occurring primordial wisdom remains as the root, as the universal ground. Its lucidity has been self-arising light from the beginning. It can neither be injured nor healed, be helped nor harmed, increased nor decreased, nor be built up nor ruined. It is beyond birth and death, rising and falling, suffering and happiness. It is beyond the need of a remedy. Thus, it is called "arising as light that is without beginning or end." This completes the nail of the thumb-sized *dharmakāya*. *Samaya!*

Fifth, the nail of the thumb-sized *dharmakāya* has three parts.

First, as the root text says, "Homage to Kun tu bZang po's self-awakened awareness that is primordially pure." The first part pertains to the homage. The meaning shows that the king of awakened awareness, *bodhicitta*, is untouched by any limits whatsoever.

Second, the expanded explanation has four parts:

(1) Explaining the essence of thumb-sized primordial awareness,

(2) Explaining the natural state of thumb-sized primordial awareness,

(3) Explaining the significance of thumb-sized primordial awareness,

(4) Explaining the reason for the expression of thumb-sized primordial awareness.

The first, [explaining the essence of thumb sized primordial awareness] has two parts:

(1) Explaining thumb-sized primordial wisdom, and

(2) Explaining thumb-sized light. (581)

First, [Explaining thumb-sized primordial wisdom] begins with the text saying, "The king of self-occurring awakened awareness is lucid." "Lucid *(gsal ba)*" here means that [awakened awareness] is without obscurations or coverings. "Self-occurring *(rang 'byung)*" refers to the fact that it is not made from causes and conditions and there is no agent that brings it forth. "Awakened awareness" *(rig pa)* here refers to the fact that this awareness serves as the basis of all [ordinary] recollections and awareness. "King" *(rgyal po)* refers to nothing being above it or coming before it, and to the fact that it stays as the ultimate realization of knowing awareness. Prior to [these ordinary recollections and awareness] there is primordial awareness and the realization of [all this] as its own play. Because it is never obscured by the non-recognition of it, in other words by delusion, it is thumb-sized primordial awareness. This is not experienced as arising from either *saṃsāra* or *nirvāṇa*. If one were to ask where it stays, the root text says, "Such that self-occurring primordial wisdom stays at its root in the universal ground." Therefore, it is not made by any causes or conditions, but rather it is self-occurring and stays from the beginning. The root text continues, "This formless primordial wisdom is devoid of color, shape, or form. This inexpressible primordial wisdom is devoid of names, words, or letters. This thought-free primordial wisdom is [devoid of] thought, analysis, or ideas." The root text refers to three things. This natural state, which is primordial wisdom's awakened awareness, because it is formless, it has no shape or color. Because it is expressionless, its basis of operation transcends names, phrases, and letters. Because primordial wisdom is thought-free and devoid of thought, analysis, or ideas, it transcends all objects of thought, analysis, or ideas. Yet, if we were to affix a name to it, as the root text says, "This thumb-sized primordial wisdom [that abides in the heart] and has no [substantial] appearance is the *dharmakāya.*" This is referred to as gShen lha dKar po [The Purest Bon Deity], but has no real designation as the universal ground. Among its numerous names it is also called "awakened awareness that is the essence-itself."

Second, [Explaining thumb-sized light]. The root text begins, "From this thumb-sized great primordial wisdom and its lucidity there arises naturally the thumb-sized great light that seems to appear." (582) From the basis of arising [universal ground] of thumb-sized primordial awareness that can arise in anyone comes a thumb-sized great light, which is the source of the visions, and stays from the beginning as self-arising. For example, from the heart of the sun, light arises in a self-arising manner. The root text continues, "This light arises in-and-by-itself in such a way that you are never separated from it or need to become integrated with it." The two—thumb-sized primordial awareness and thumb-sized light—remain individually and are not condensed into a single [phenomenon to become integrated with]. Yet, because they remain as one, you are never separated from either, individually. They remain from the beginning as self-arising in themselves. The root text says, "With respect to its lucidity, this [light] appears as insubstantial and without inherent nature." This means that this thumb-sized light is lucid and clear, yet is explained as being without independent existence as a real thing and without [definable] characteristics. The root text continues, "It is without form or color, and without any partiality." This means that this thumb-sized light is the basis of arising of all forms—the enlightened bodies of *Buddhas*, the ordinary bodies of sentient beings, etc. While this is just the way it is, the essence is such that forms arise impartially everywhere. This light is also the basis of arising of all colors of light—white, green, red, blue light, etc. While this is just the way it is, the essence is such that colors arise impartially everywhere. The root text continues, "It is beyond a measure of any size, like large or small, and any measure of weight." This means that the greatness of this thumb-sized light is beyond measure. It stays in its real nature as space, without edge or center. Likewise, its smallness is beyond measure, just like it is possible for the tiniest of creatures to enter the body through the eyes. The root text continues, "It is called, 'the great appearance of the *dharmakāya*.' It is also called the root deity who is given the designation gShen lha dKar po [The Purest Bon Deity]. Among its numerous names it is called 'the awakened awareness that appears through special insight.'" (583)

Second, [Explaining the] natural state of this thumb-sized primordial wisdom, the root text says, "Whenever the divine eyes of primordial wisdom arise with respect to this thumb-sized *dharmakāya*...." This refers to the fact that this thumb-sized light is referred to as a "body" because it is unchanging. Furthermore, with respect to this thumb-sized primordial wisdom, the root text also says, "These divine eyes are never covered by obscuration." These two are inseparable, body and primordial wisdom, and are said to be non-dual. When the root text says, "It sees everywhere," it means seeing in all ten directions; and when it says, "but its enlightened body has neither front nor back," it means that this enlightened body and this thumb-sized primordial wisdom have no front or back with respect to the true face of primordial wisdom. It is lucid in all ten directions like a crystal egg. The root text continues, "Without looking, it sees everywhere. These divine eyes are never covered by obscuration." Because no obscurations exist with respect to the eyes of awakened awareness, everything is lucid, even without looking, like a mirror that is spotless and pure. The root text continues, "Everything arises as the great transparency without outside or inside and remains as all-pervasiveness." This refers to the fact that this thumb-sized primordial wisdom neither abides outside nor does it abide inside. In general, it abides without being caught up [in distinctions] like outside and inside.

The root text continues, "...without edge or center. It stays all-pervasive and all-encompassing." This means that this thumb-sized primordial wisdom is without any limitations, one-sidedness, or partialities. It remains without edges or center, cardinal or intermediate directions, or partialization. The root text continues, "...and arises in the [expanse of the] universal ground unstained by anything whatsoever." This means that this thumb-sized primordial wisdom is the basis of arising of everything, such as *saṃsāra* and *nirvāṇa*, *Buddhas* and sentient beings, suffering and compassion, conceptual thought and primordial wisdom, virtue and sin, happiness and suffering, container and contents, body and mind, sense-object and its knowing, (584) cause and effect, higher and lower realms of re-birth, etc. Yet, even though it remains just as it is, these distinctions remain without being touched by any limitations.

Third, explaining the significance of thumb-sized primordial awareness is as follows: The root text begins, "Primordially staying, it [nevertheless] arises as the play of the previously mentioned king of awakened awareness. Here [in this primordial condition] there is no *saṃsāra* or *nirvāṇa*, no cycles of time..." This refers to thumb-sized primordial wisdom, the king of awakened awareness, which stays as self-arising from the beginning, with nothing whatsoever brought into existence, such as the phenomena of *saṃsāra* and the phenomena of *nirvāṇa*, the nine cycles of time, the three realms, the five elements, etc. The root text continues, "...just the occurrence of the king of awakened awareness in the primordial ground." This means that before anything came into existence this king of awakened awareness has remained from the beginning. The root text continues, "Here, [primordially] there is no accomplishment of *Buddhahood* nor any mandate to become a *Buddha*." This means that before the play of thumb-sized primordial wisdom, which is the king of awakened awareness, there was no making of *Buddhas* because this thumb-sized primordial wisdom did not exist in terms of the precepts of gShen rab [disciples of Bon]. Also, before the play of that, there did not exist what are called sentient beings, because the thumb-sized primordial wisdom did not yet produce the karmic actions of sentient beings. Before that, there was no individual who was the agent, nor was there anything produced by such individuals. Before the play of that, there was no experiencing of the production of a cause of attachment, nor any co-emergent conditions, nor was there any integration of these causes and conditions with respect to thumb-sized primordial wisdom. Before the play of it, there was no experience of the making of the causes of the seemingly external world, namely the most subtle particles, (585) because this thumb-sized primordial wisdom had not yet experienced attachment to the seeming appearances of the external world. Before the play of that, there was no production of what are referred to as the five causal elements because that thumb-sized primordial wisdom had not yet a body made of these elements. Before the play of that, there was no experience of the production of sperm by the father nor the womb of the mother because this thumb-sized primordial wisdom did not yet experience the birth of causes, which would have been the white and red vital essences [from each parent]. Before the play of that, there was no experience of the primordial wisdom of realization, nor the failure to recognize awakened awareness, which is delusion, because this thumb-sized primordial wisdom had not yet experienced *saṁsāra* or *nirvāṇa*.

If you were to ask how this stays in whatever way it does, the root text says, "Here, this self-occurring primordial wisdom remains as the root, as the universal ground." This means that it is not made of any causes or conditions, but primordial wisdom stays from the beginning as self occurring and self-arising.

Fourth, explaining the reason for the expression "thumb-sized primordial awareness" is as follows: If you were to ask how to speak about this thumb-sized primordial wisdom's self-awakened awareness, the root text says, "Its lucidity has been self-arising light from the beginning. It can neither be injured nor healed, helped nor harmed, increased nor decreased, nor be built up nor ruined. It is beyond birth and death, rising and falling, suffering or happiness. It is beyond the need of a remedy." This thumb-sized primordial wisdom is self-arising as lucid as light from the very beginning. It is thumb-sized because it cannot be injured by demons. It is thumb-sized because it cannot be healed by gods. It is thumb-sized because it cannot be imputed with the benefits of favorable conditions. (586) It is thumb-sized because it cannot be imputed with the harms of unfavorable conditions. It is thumb-sized because it cannot proliferate into many things. It is thumb-sized because it cannot be reduced into few things. It is thumb-sized because it cannot be constructed. It is thumb-sized because it cannot be spoiled by effort. It is thumb-sized because it is without the causes of re-birth. It is thumb-sized because it is without the conditions of dying. It is thumb-sized because it is not enhanced by youth. It is thumb-sized because it is not diminished by aging. It is thumb-sized because it is without happiness due to [purification of] the elements or suffering due to attachment. It is thumb-sized because it cannot be destroyed or conquered by remedies. As the root text says, "Thus, it is called 'arising as light that is without beginning or end'."

Third, the conclusion is clearly expressed in the root text, "This completes the nail of the thumb-sized *dharmakāya*."

6: The Nail of Awakened Awareness-itself, which is the Completion Body [*Sambhogakāya*], i.e., Unification

Homage to Kun tu bZang po, whose self-awakened awareness is the Completion Body [*sambhogakāya*]. From within the vast expanse of the universal ground that is clarity/emptiness, and without any [independently existing] identity, thumb-sized primordial wisdom arises, lucid in-itself and free of conceptual thought. [Both] the expanse and primordial wisdom stay as non-dual sameness [everywhere]. The three kinds of visions [sound, light, and rays] arise from this, whose real nature is liveliness. The seeming [sense] objects and awakened awareness are neither separate nor mixed. All such seeming visions and sounds, and likewise, particular concepts, are complete, without exception. This is the treasury of the Great Completion wherein the expanse and primordial wisdom are unified. (555) This is the treasury of the Great Completion wherein space and the domain of space are unified. This is the treasury of the Great Completion wherein skillful means and sublime knowledge are unified. This is the treasury of the Great Completion wherein object and consciousness are unified. This is the treasury of the Great Completion wherein cause and effect are unified. This is the treasury of the Great Completion wherein body and mind are unified. This is the treasury of the Great Completion wherein container and

contained are unified. This is the treasury of the Great Completion wherein male and female are unified. This is the treasury of the Great Completion wherein enlightened bodies and primordial wisdom are unified. This is the treasury of the Great Completion wherein deities and their celestial palaces are unified. This completes the nail of the Completion Body and its Unification. *Samaya!*

With respect to the sixth nail, unification, the Completion Body [*sambhogakāya*], there are three parts.

First is the homage as the root text says, "Homage to Kun tu bZang po, whose self-awakened awareness is the Completion Body [*sambhogakāya*]." This passage explains the homage. It means that with respect to *bodhicitta*, everything within *saṃsāra* and *nirvāṇa* without exception is brought to completion.

Second, as for the extensive explanation there is a brief version and a more detailed version. The brief version has two parts—the basis of completion and the manner of completion.

First [the basis of completion] is as follows: The root text says, "From within the vast expanse of the universal ground, that is clarity/emptiness, and without any [independently existing] identity...." This passage illustrates the expanse of the universal ground. When the root text says, "Thumb-sized primordial wisdom arises lucid in itself and free of conceptual thought," it explains primordial wisdom's awakened awareness. Then the root text says, "[Both] the expanse and primordial wisdom stay as non-dual sameness [everywhere]." The meaning of this passage refers to the fact that the universal ground and awakened awareness are without duality. (587) When whatever arises is complete, it is complete with respect to the basis, which is the non-duality of the universal ground and awakened awareness.

Second, the manner of completion is as follows: When whatever arises is complete, it means that it is complete [encompassing] all of *saṃsāra* and *nirvāṇa* without exception. Furthermore, the root text says, "The three kinds of visions [sound, light, and rays] arise from this, whose real nature is liveliness." These three visions are the root of everything [purified] in *saṃsāra* and *nirvāṇa*. Ultimate sound, light, and light-rays are the three great visions. Every one of these is free of being made to happen, and is self-arising as spontaneously present and complete. The root text continues, "The seeming [sense] objects and awakened awareness are neither separate nor mixed." This means that with respect to the three—ultimate sound, light, and light-rays—they are referring to the appearing objects [or visions], and with respect to primordial wisdom's awakened awareness, this refers to the subject who knows them. These two—the object [the visions] and the subject, the awakened awareness [that knows]—are not separated and yet are not mixed, but remain as an inseparable [non-dual] pair. As they are not mixed together, their individual characteristics remain lucid. The root text continues, "All such seeming visions and sounds, and likewise, particular concepts, are complete, without exception." This means that with respect to *bodhicitta*, they are complete in their own way as the five lights of the visions. They are also complete as the five causal elements of the visions. Being complete [with respect to the causal elements], they are therefore complete with respect to all the seeming appearances of *saṁsāra* and *nirvāṇa* without exception. Furthermore, all the visions of *nirvāṇa* —the celestial palaces, the pure realms, the *mandalas* and their ornaments, the colors of the bodies, the *mudras*, the major and minor marks, the principal deities, their retinues and emanations, the five enlightened *Buddha* bodies, the five deity families, etc.—all these pure visions are complete as spontaneously present without effort [to produce them]. Likewise, all the seeming appearances of *saṁsāra*, including the external container and the internal nectar of contents—its living beings, cycles of time, worlds, the living places of the six classes of beings and the *mandalas* of the three realms, the five elements, the five aggregates, (588) the five poisons, the internal organs and five containers [within the body], the five limbs, the five sense-systems, the five sense-organs, the five sense-objects, etc.—all these impure seeming appearances are complete as spontaneously present without effort [to produce them]. With respect to *bodhicitta*, the sounds that are the root of what is heard are complete in their own way, and in being complete this way, the sounds of external elements, the sounds of internal awakened awareness, the emanation of the sacred speech of the *Buddhas*, the speech and symbolic communication of sentient beings, etc., all of these particular sounds, however many are heard, without exception, are complete as spontaneously present without any effort [to produce them]. With respect to *bodhicitta*, the light-rays that are the root of what is thought are complete in their own way. The 10,000 and the 100,000 manifestations of primordial wisdom of the complete *Buddhas*, and also the 84,000 particular conceptual thoughts of sentient beings, etc., however many of these particular objects can be known by subjects, without exception are complete as spontaneously present without any effort [to produce them].

Second, with respect to the extensive explanation, this explanation comes from the teachings on the ten unifications [or the ten treasuries of the Great Completion].

The root text [begins the list of these when it] says, "This is the treasury of the Great Completion wherein the expanse and primordial wisdom are unified." This means that with respect to the three great visions, it is referred to as "the expanse," and with respect to awakened awareness, it is referred to as primordial wisdom['s liveliness]. Because these are never divided or separated, they are referred to as being unified. With respect to this unification, because everything in *samsāra* and *nirvāṇa* without exception is complete, it is called "complete." Because it is immeasurable, it is called, "great." Because everything in *samsāra* and *nirvāṇa* arises from it without exception, it is called "treasury."

The root text continues, "This is the treasury of the Great Completion wherein space and the domain of space are unified." With respect to the three visions, it is referred to as the "domain [of space wherein they arise]." With respect to primordial wisdom's awakened awareness, it is referred to as "space." Because these two are never divided or separated, they are referred to as "space and domain of space as being unified." (589) The meaning of Great Completion and treasury have been described previously.

The root text continues, "This is the treasury of the Great Completion wherein skillful means and knowledge are unified." This means that with respect to the three visions it is referred to as the "expanse of great knowledge," and with respect to primordial wisdom's awakened awareness it is referred to as "the space of great skillful means." The meaning of unification, etc. has been explained before.

The root text continues, "This is the treasury of the Great Completion wherein object and consciousness are unified." This means that with respect to the three visions it is referred to as "the object to be known," and all seemingly external appearances arise from these [visions]. With respect to primordial wisdom's awakened awareness, it is referred to as the "knowing subject," and all the particular ways of knowing that are internally known by a subject arise from that. The meaning of unification, etc. has been explained before.

The root text continues, "This is the treasury of the Great Completion wherein cause and effect are unified." With respect to the three visions, this is referred to as the "cause," and with respect to primordial wisdom's awakened awareness, this is referred to as "fruition." All phenomena that are subsumed under cause and effect arise from that.

The root text continues, "This is the treasury of the Great Completion wherein body and mind are unified." With respect to the three visions, it is referred to as "body," and all the emanations of bodies, however many there may be, arise from that. With respect to primordial wisdom's awakened awareness, it is called "mind," and all the emanations of mind, however many there may be, arise from that. The meaning of unification, etc. is similar to that mentioned previously.

The root text continues, "This is the treasury of the Great Completion wherein container and contained are unified." With respect to the three visions, it is referred to as the "container," and all the seeming external appearances of the world arise from that. With respect to primordial wisdom's awakened awareness, it is referred to as the "contents," in that all the seeming internal contents of the minds of all sentient beings arise from that. (590) The meaning of unification, etc. is similar to that mentioned previously.

The root text continues, "This is the treasury of the Great Completion wherein male and female are unified." With respect to the three visions, it is referred to as "female," in that it is the queen of all phenomena, much like how rainbows appear from the expanse as a manifestation of the sun. With respect to awakened awareness, the male, the king of skillful means, it is referred to as "primordial wisdom's awakened awareness in space." These two have no separations or divisions so they are referred to as being "unified." The meaning of unification, etc. is similar to that mentioned previously.

The root text continues, "This is the treasury of the Great Completion wherein the enlightened bodies and primordial wisdom are unified." With respect to the three visions, it is referred to as "the enlightened bodies," as all the emanations of bodies, however many there may be, arise from that. With respect to awakened awareness, it is called "primordial wisdom." The meaning of unification, etc. is similar to that mentioned previously.

The root text continues, "This is the treasury of the Great Completion wherein deities and their celestial palaces are unified." With respect to the three visions, it is referred to as the "celestial palace," and all outer, inner, and secret *mandalas* arise from that. With respect to primordial wisdom's awakened awareness, it is referred to as gShen lha dKar po, the root deity, and all outer, inner, and secret assemblies of deities, and also the assemblies of deities of the four kinds of enlightened activities, arise from that. Because these two have no separations or divisions they are referred to as being "unified." Because they are complete, without exception, they are referred to as "complete." Because they are immeasurable they are referred to as "great." Since everything arises from this, it is referred to as "treasury."

Third, the meaning of the conclusion is conveyed by the text when it says, "This completes the nail of the Completion Body and its unification."

7: The Nail of Self-Awakened Awareness that is the Impartial Emanation Bodies [*Nirmānakāyas*]

Homage to Kun tu bZang po's self-awakened awareness that is the Emanation Bodies [*nirmānakāyas*]. Both the appearing objects and primordial wisdom's awakened awareness are neither separate nor mixed. They are liveliness, which is unified [as a non-dual pair]. [From this liveliness, all] the visions and sounds, and particular conceptual thoughts arise without exception. The various appearances, from the interdependence of six sense-consciousnesses, six sense-organs, and six sense-objects, arise throughout *samsāra* and

nirvāna as emanations, without preference. Not engaging anything, these arise as self-occurring liveliness. With respect to the expanse wherein these visions [self-occur] they arise without end and without ever being diminished. In this space, awakened awareness is lucid, never obscured. Whatever occurs in-and-by-itself is liberated in-and-by-itself and comes to completion as a single sphere of ultimate reality [wherein everything is interconnected]. This completes the nail of the impartial Emanation Bodies [*nirmānakāyas*]. *Samaya!*

Seventh, with respect to the nail of the impartial Emanation Bodies [*nirmānakāyas*], there are three parts.

First, the root text gives the homage. (591) It says, "Homage to Kun tu bZang po's self-awakened awareness-itself that is the Emanation Bodies [*nirmānakāyas*]." The meaning refers to the fact that the magical display of *bodhicitta* can arise anywhere, and that this [*bodhicitta*] is the agent of everything.

Second, the extensive explanation has two parts, a brief explanation and a more extensive explanation.

First, the brief explanation begins when the root text says, "Both the appearing objects and primordial wisdom's awakened awareness are neither separate nor mixed. They are liveliness, which is unified [as a non-dual pair]." This refers to both the three objects—ultimate sound, light, and light-rays—and also to the subject—primordial wisdom's awakened awareness. From the inseparableness of these, and from the liveliness of their unification, the entire magical display of *samsāra* and *nirvāna* arises, without exception. Whatever arises is referred to in the root text in the passage, "[From this liveliness, all] the visions and sounds, and particular conceptual thoughts arise without exception." As explained previously these are the occasions of the Completion Body. From the light and from the liveliness of awakened awareness, all the various seeming appearances of *samsāra* and *nirvāna* arise. From ultimate sound and also from the liveliness of awakened awareness, all the speech of *Buddhas,* as well as the particular speech of ordinary sentient beings, without exception, arises. From light-rays and from the liveliness of awakened awareness, the primordial wisdom that is the omniscience of the *Buddhas*, as well as all the particular conceptual thoughts of sentient beings, without exception, arises.

Second, there is a more extensive explanation. The root text begins, "The various appearances, from the interdependence of six sense-consciousnesses, six sense-organs, and six sense-objects...." From the magical display of *bodhicitta*, internally, there arise the seeming appearances of the six consciousnesses—the eye consciousness, ear consciousness, etc., and externally, there arise the six sense-objects, such as sights, sounds, smells, tastes, and sensations. In between there arise the six sense-organs such as eye, nose, etc., and here is the connection between body and mind (592). The root text continues, "[They] arise throughout *saṃsāra* and *nirvāṇa* as emanations, without preference." This refers to how the various sense-consciousnesses, sense-objects, and sense-organs arise from liveliness when there is no realization, so that they arise as the various emanations of *saṃsāra* without preferences and impartially. Yet, when there is realization they arise as the various emanations of *nirvāṇa*. The root text continues, "Not engaging anything, these arise as self-occurring liveliness." This means that they arise from *bodhicitta*. This magical display of *saṃsāra* and *nirvāṇa* is without any purposeful doing, and thus it arises as self-occurring and self-arising. The root text continues, "With respect to the expanse wherein these visions [self-occur] they arise without end and without ever being diminished. In this space, awakened awareness is lucid, never obscured." This means that with respect to *bodhicitta* the magical displays of *saṃsāra* and *nirvāṇa* arise just the way they are. With respect to these three great visions, they never end or diminish the way the smallest particles do not diminish. With respect to primordial wisdom's awakened awareness moment-by-moment, it is lucid and free of obscuration. The root text continues, "Whatever occurs in-and-by-itself is liberated in-and-by-itself and comes to completion as a single sphere of ultimate reality." This means that even though the magical displays of *saṃsāra* and *nirvāṇa* arise just as they are, nevertheless, they do not come from anywhere else nor do they go anywhere else. They occur, but they occur from the domain of space of the mind. They become liberated, but they become liberated from the domain of space of the mind. Everything is complete in the single sphere of ultimate reality of mind [wherein everything is interconnected].

Third, the meaning of the conclusion is clear when the root text says, "This completes the nail of the impartial Emanation Bodies [*nirmāṇakāyas*]."

8: The Nail that Eliminates the Darkness of Doubt Through Illustrative Examples

Homage to Kun tu bZang po, who eliminates the darkness of doubt. Illustrative examples show the unified connection between a sense-object and awakened awareness, such as the light [reflected on water like] a water-moon, [or radiating from] the sun, and [emanating from] a butter lamp. There are four occasions—staying [in the universal ground], the union [of body and mind at the beginning of life], the separation [of the mind from the body at death], and the delusion [that arises in the after-death states]. [Each of these four conditions] can be free of obscuration, having obscuration (556), having clarity, or having dullness. By seeing this in-and-by-itself, and by means of this, the liberation of *Buddhahood* comes. Gaining mastery over the visions turns the wheel of self-mastery.

Sentient beings, by virtue of seeing things other than what they really are, become deluded. Chasing after these visions as if they were something other than what they really are, is to be influenced and deceived by illusion. Without karmic cause, these visions occur by the force of their own real nature. They have arisen without the full measure of time, without beginning or end. Make a determination about this heart-essence [of the mind] free of delusion and there will be no more delusion. Coming to the ultimate determination regarding these visions, you will not be deceived by [seeing these visions as externally existing] appearances. This completes the nail of illustrative examples. *Samaya!*

Eight, the nail of illustrative examples has three parts.

First, is the homage. The root text says, "Homage to Kun tu bZang po, who eliminates the darkness of doubt." (593) This shows the offering of the homage. This refers to when one recognizes *bodhicitta*, makes a decisive determination about it, and has confidence about this determination, so that the darkness of doubt is purified in-and-by-itself.

Second, is the extensive explanation. It has five parts:

(1) Using illustrative examples to show the connection between the appearing object and primordial wisdom's awakened awareness,

(2) Showing the way lucidity and obscuration come on four occasions,

(3) Showing the way liberation and delusion come,

(4) Showing the way of causation and time, and

(5) Showing the way to eradicate delusion.

First, as the root text says, "Illustrative examples show the unified connection between a sense-object and awakened awareness, such as the light [reflected on water like] a water-moon, [or radiating from] the sun, and [emanating from] a butter lamp." Here, awakened awareness is likened to water. The three visions—ultimate sound, light, and light-rays—are likened to the way light [is reflected on] the water. Awakened awareness is also likened to a crystal. The three visions are likened to the light from the crystal. Awakened awareness is likened to the sun. The three visions are likened to light [rays from the sun]. Awakened awareness is likened to a butter lamp. The three visions are likened to the way the light [is emitted from] the butter lamp.

Second, showing the way lucidity and obscuration come on four occasions. The root text says, "There are four occasions—staying [in the universal ground], the union [of body and mind at the beginning of life], the separation [of the mind from the body at death], and the delusion [that arises in the after-death states]." Staying refers to the occasion of staying in the universal ground and primordial wisdom. The union refers to the coming together of body and mind in this lifetime. Separation refers to how the body and mind each become free from each other at the occasion of the arising of the after-death state of the clear-light of the *dharmadhātu*. Delusion refers to the occasion of wandering in the after-death state of existence. The root text continues, "[Each of these four conditions] can be free of obscuration, having obscuration, (556) having clarity, or having dullness." Whenever there is staying in the universal ground and primordial awareness, awakened awareness is like the sun arising in a cloudless sky. The three—ultimate sound, light, and light-rays (594)—stay without obscuration. Yet, at this present moment, when the body and mind have been connected, awakened awareness is like a butter lamp placed inside a pot. Having been obscured by the body, it remains there having become obscured. When the body and mind have become separated [at the time of death], this is when the after-death state of clear-light arises, and awakened awareness is like the sun in a cloudless sky. It arises clearly for the first time in this after-death state. During the occasion of the after-death state of existence [or rebirth], awakened awareness arises like the sun covered by clouds, and awakened awareness becomes obscured by the appearance of delusion.

Third, showing the way liberation and delusion come is as follows: The root text begins, "Seeing this in-and-by-itself, and by means of this, the liberation of *Buddhahood* comes." Because Kun tu bZang po knew that these three visions—ultimate sound, light, and light-rays—were self-appearing, he had *Buddhahood* from the very beginning without any need for a master to teach him. The root text continues, "Gaining mastery over the visions turns the wheel of self-mastery." This means that because Kun tu bZang po knew that these visions were self-appearing, he did not chase after these visions. Because he did not chase after them, he gained mastery with respect to these visions. Since he gained mastery, he is able to transform these visions over and over again into whatever is fitting to the situation. For example, he is like a king who is able to bring an entire country under his control. The root text continues, "Sentient beings, by virtue of seeing things other than what they really are, become deluded." This refers to the fact that sentient beings of the three realms do not know that the three visions—ultimate sound, light, and light-rays—are self-arising. Because they see these visions as independently existing external appearances existing outside of their own mind-streams, being without a guide they erroneously wander in *saṁsāra*. The root text continues, "Chasing after these visions as if they were something other than what they really are, is to be influenced and deceived by illusion." Because sentient beings of the three realms see these visions as some other appearance, they chase after these visions. Because they chase after these visions, (595) awakened awareness loses its own force. Because awakened awareness loses its own force, the visions become something other. For example, it is like a king wandering among common people or like a child chasing after a rainbow.

Fourth, showing the way of causation and time is as follows: The root text says, "Without karmic cause, these visions occur by the force of their own real nature." Kung tu bZang po realized *Buddhahood* without having a master. Sentient beings of the three realms erroneously wander in *saṃsāra* without a guide. If you were to ask what had happened in previous times with respect to the causes and conditions of virtue and sin, it would be the case that nothing happened with respect to the causes and conditions of virtue and sin. These just seem to occur from the liveliness of the natural state and as such have their own force. For example, it is like tongues of flame rising upward and like drops of water falling downward by their own force without an agent [making it happen]. The root text continues, "They have arisen without the full measure of time, without beginning or end." This refers to the fact that Kun tu bZang po has realization and sentient beings of the three realms are deluded. If you were to ask how long this full measure of time might be, there is no measure of time [in the natural state]. This is referred to as "the three times arising without beginning or end."

Fifth, showing the way to eradicate delusion is as follows: The root text begins, "Make a determination about the heart-essence [of the mind] free of delusion, and there will be no more delusion." This means that if you have recognized the natural state, which is awakened awareness in its original purity, and then have come to make a decisive determination about that, then delusion no longer exists. For example, it is like the son of a king who eventually ends up seated on the throne. The root text continues, "Coming to the ultimate determination regarding these visions, you will not be deceived by [seeing these visions and externally existing] appearances." This means that if, having penetrated the three—ultimate sound, light, and light-rays—and the causes and conditions [which make them seem real], and then you recognize them as self-arising, then you will never come to be deceived by these three visions again. (596) For example, if you know an illusion as an illusion, then you are not deceived by illusions again, or if you know that a rainbow is without any real nature, you don't chase after the rainbow after that.

Third, the conclusion is explained clearly in the root text when it says, "This completes the nail of illustrative examples. *Samaya!*"

9: The Nail of the Depths of Self-Awakened Awareness Without Uniting With or Separating From It

Homage to Kun tu bZang po's self-awakened awareness, without [either] uniting with or separating from it. Primordial wisdom's self-awakened awareness is hidden and concealed. It stays in the universal base in the [physical] heart, like the expanse of space and like an ocean. With respect to the heart of light [that is the basis] of the visions, it [stays] like an offering tent of five kinds of rainbow light. With respect to the physical heart, it is like a pot filled with semi-precious jewels. With respect to the thumb-sized primordial wisdom [that shines forth in its] lucidity, it is like a butter lamp inside the pot. With respect to the three—sound, light, and light-rays—they are like the liveliness of the light-rays [radiating] from the butter lamp.

The king of awakened awareness arises from within the depths [of the physical heart space]. It arises from within the emptiness of the universal base.

The visions arise from the interior of this light [in the physical heart]. The illusions arise within the middle of the body. As for its outer aspect, it arises in-and-by-itself in the center of the heart. As for its inner aspect, it arises in-and-by-itself in the interior space of the five lights. As for its secret aspect, it arises in-and-by-itself from within the domain of the universal ground. This is the source of everything occurring as very pure. This is the treasury of space. [Yet,] there are so many ways [awakened awareness] gradually becomes contaminated and obscured. If there is no gateway [for awakened awareness because of obscuration] you do not come to see them [the visions]. Yet, [once] opening the gateway to this treasury, the innermost treasury becomes manifest. This completes the nail of the depths of self-awakened awareness. *Samaya!*

The ninth nail pertains to the arising of awakened awareness in-and-by-itself in the depths [of one's heart]. There are three parts. The first part in the root text is the homage, "Homage to Kun tu bZang po's self-awakened awareness, without [either] union or separation." This passage gives the homage. This passage shows that since *bodhicitta* does not comes from anywhere, it does not come from uniting with anything. Since it does not go anywhere it cannot be separated from anything. This means that [*bodhicitta* is really] spontaneously present and co-emergent with the three times.

Second, the extensive explanation is as follows: The root text begins, "Primordial wisdom's awakened awareness-itself is hidden and concealed." Primordial wisdom's awakened awareness is said to be "hidden" because it is difficult to realize, and said to be "concealed" because it is [typically] covered by obscurations. Where is it hidden? According to the root text, "It stays in the universal base in the [physical] heart, like the expanse of space and like an ocean." Here [the author] is speaking about the expanse of the universal ground. Primordial wisdom's awakened awareness is within the space-like expanse of the universal base. Primordial wisdom's awakened awareness is hidden there like the stars [that cannot be seen] in the daytime. Within this ocean-like expanse of the universal base, primordial wisdom's awakened awareness is hidden like a turtle with its limbs contracted inside its body.

The root text continues, "With respect to the heart of light [the basis] of the visions, it [stays] like an offering tent of five kinds of rainbow light." [The author] is speaking here of the five lights [much like the colored canopy] of an offering tent. Primordial wisdom's awakened awareness is within the interior of these five lights, but is obscured and hidden in-and-by-itself (597) by its own inherent light.

The root text continues, "With respect to the physical heart, it is like a pot filled with semi-precious jewels." Here [the author] is speaking about how the [physical] heart is like a dark purple offering tent made of quartz. Here, in the center of this offering tent of quartz in the heart, primordial wisdom's awakened awareness is concealed, much like placing a butter lamp in a [closed] pot. The root text continues, "With respect

to the thumb-sized primordial wisdom [that shines forth in its] lucidity,
it is like a butter lamp inside the pot." This passage uses a metaphor to
show how primordial wisdom's awakened awareness arises from inside
[of the heart]. The root text continues, "With respect to the three—
sound, light, and light-rays—they are like the liveliness of the light-rays
[radiating] from the butter lamp." This passage uses the [same] metaphor to show how the three great visions arise in-and-by-themselves
with respect to primordial wisdom's awakened awareness [in the heart].
The root text continues, "The king of awakened awareness arises from
within the depths [of the physical heart space]." This passage explains
how awakened awareness arises from within [this heart-space]. When
it arises from within something, the root text means that "it arises from
within the emptiness of the universal base. The visions arise from the
interior of this light [in the physical heart]. The illusions arise within the
middle of the body." The text continues, "As for its outer aspect, it arises
in-and-by-itself in the center of the heart." This means that externally it
arises in-and-by-itself from the center of the heart. Internally, it arises-
in-and-by-itself from the interior of the five lights. Secretly, it arises in-
and-by-itself from within the space-like domain of the universal ground.
The root text continues, "This is the source of everything occurring as
very pure. This is the treasury of space." This passage refers to all the
positive qualities of the universal ground and awakened awareness [that
arise]. The line, "the source of everything" refers to being the source of
all phenomena of *saṃsāra* and *nirvāṇa* without exception. "Very pure" refers to it being without any stains whatsoever. "Treasury of space" refers
to all the possible endless qualities that arise from it.

The root text continues, "[Yet,] there are so many ways [awak-
ened awareness] gradually becomes contaminated and obscured." This
passage refers to the fault of not realizing the universal ground and
awakened awareness. If these are not realized in their outer aspect for
whatever reason, then they are not realized because they have become
obscured by the body, (598) much like when a butter lamp is placed inside [a sealed] pot. If these are not realized in their inner aspect for
whatever reason, then they are not realized because they have become
obscured by the seeming external appearances of the six sense-objects,

much like when the stars cannot be seen in the daytime. If they are not realized secretly for whatever reason, then they are not realized because they have become obscured by the habitual karmic propensities of the mind, much like the sun obscured by clouds. The root text continues, "If there is no gateway [for awakened awareness because of obscuration] you do not come to see them." Thus, the universal ground and awakened awareness have gradually become obscured by many types of obscurations. Externally, if there is no gateway to the instructions, you will not see the innermost truth of the *dharmadhātu*. Internally, if there is no gateway to the lamps, you will not come to see the innermost truth of the three visions—ultimate sound, light, and light-rays. Secretly, if there is no gateway to awakened awareness, you will not come to see the innermost truth of the universal ground. The root text continues, "Yet, [once] opening the gateway to this treasury, the innermost treasury becomes manifest." This means that the universal ground and awakened awareness have been realized. Externally, when the gateway of this treasury of instructions is opened, the innermost treasury of *dharmadhātu* is shown. Internally, when the gateway of this treasury of the lamps is opened, the innermost treasury of the three visions—ultimate sound, light, and light-rays are shown. Secretly, when the gateway of the treasury of primordial wisdom's awakened awareness is opened, the innermost treasury of the expanse of the universal ground is shown.

The conclusion is clearly expressed in the root text when it says, "This completes the nail of the depths of awakened awareness-itself. *Samaya!*"

10: The Nail of the Self-Awakened Awareness that Uncovers the Straight Unmistaken Path

Homage to Kun tu bZang po, whose self-awakened awareness is the straight unmistaken [path]. (557) From thumb-sized primordial wisdom's self-awakened awareness the five kinds of radiant light of the visions arise. From them the five kinds of [pure] elemental energies arise. From them the five kinds of [impure] dregs arise. Mind and body are generated from these twenty-five.

Awakened awareness arises from the pathways of the channels. When it arises upwards this is the pathway of *nirvāna*. When it arises downwards this is the pathway of *samsāra*. When it arises from the right [main side channel] this is the path of faults. When it arises from the left [main side channel] this is the path of positive qualities. The three gateways are the path of the three realms of *samsāra*. Arising at the four gateways are the paths of the four kinds of birth. Arising at the five gateways are the paths of the five states of being. Arising at the nine gateways [orifices] are the paths of the nine levels [of practice]. However, the central [channel] is the path wherein samsara and nirvana become non-dual.

The king of awakened awareness arises from this path. [At first], it arises from the empty expanse of the universal ground. Then, it arises as the light of the visions from the interior [of the *kati* tube channel]. Finally, it arises as realization in the central channel [and once integrated] into the mind-stream it arises from [the eye lamps]. This is the natural path of primordial, unadulterated awakened awareness. This is the path of supreme primordial wisdom and its lucidity. This is the unmistaken path of the energy drops. Here, there is no gateway to the path of *samsāra*. Awakened awareness is like the person riding the horse and the mind; the recollections and sense-mind is like the horse. [Awakened awareness] moves without any hindrances [as if riding along] by virtue of the winds. In the central channel, the path of realization comes to completion once coming to the secret gateway of bliss [crown chakra] at the crown of the head. Here, the king of awakened awareness arises nakedly, and the layer of conceptual thought is stripped off. Here, is where the face of self-occurring primordial wisdom is seen. Here, the darkness of not recognizing awakened awareness and delusion is purified. Here, the gateways to the three realms [of *samsāra*] and the nine levels [of practice] are stirred up and the path of the five poisons and afflictive emotions is cut off. Here, the ocean of *samsāra* and the six types of beings dries up. Here, the gateways to the four kinds of births within *samsāra* are emptied out. Here, the three-fold embodiment of enlightenment arises in-and-by-itself continuously. This completes the nail of the unmistaken path. (558) *Samaya!*

There are three parts to the nail of the straight, unmistaken path.

First, when the root text says, "Homage to Kun tu bZang po, whose self-awakened awareness is the straight unmistaken [path]," it refers to the homage. This means that if there is realization of the ultimate truth of *bodhicitta*, without constructions or adulterations regarding its inherent nature, (599) then this is the straight, unmistaken path.

Second, the extensive explanation has three parts:

(1) Explaining the way by which the body and mind are generated from the five lights and the five elements,

(2) Explaining the way awakened awareness arises in the path of the energy channels, and

(3) Explaining the way of consciousness-transference in the path of the central channel.

First, [explaining the way by which the body and mind are generated from the five lights and the five elements] is as follows: The root text begins, "From thumb-sized primordial wisdom's awakened awareness-itself the five kinds of radiant light of the visions arises. From them the five kinds of [pure] elemental energies arise. From them the five kinds of [impure] dregs arise. Mind and body are generated from the twenty-five." This explains how from the thumb-sized primordial wisdom the five lights arise, and from the five lights the five elemental energies arise, and from the five elemental energies the five residually impure elements arise, and from these the twenty-five elemental energies—either pure or impure—arise. Furthermore, by means of these five kinds of lights—the space light, the wind light, the fire light, the water light, and the earth light—the supports for the body and mind are created and thoroughly generated. By means of the five types of gases—the gaseous nature of space, the gaseous nature of wind, the gaseous nature of fire, the gaseous nature of water, and the gaseous nature of earth—the body and mind are combined into a single entity and are revitalized and nourished. By means of the five types of warmth—the warmth of space, the warmth of wind, the warmth of fire, the warmth of water, and the warmth of earth—the body and mind are completely caused to ripen. By means of the five aspects—the wind of space, the wind of wind, the wind of fire, the wind of water, and the wind of earth—the pure and residually impure elements of the body and mind are caused to become purified in the interior of the central channel. The way by which the body and mind arise from the five kinds of elements and develop (600) is explained in the *Byang chub sems kyi gnad drug* [*Six Essential Points of Bodhicitta*].

Second, explaining the way awakened awareness arises in the path of the energy channels has two parts:

(1) The teachings about the faults and positive qualities on the path,

(2) The teachings about the non-duality of the faults and positive qualities on the path.

As the root text begins, "Awakened awareness arises from the pathways of the channels." This means that the [central] channel is the gateway for awakened awareness. The root text continues, "When it arises upwards this is the pathway of *nirvāṇa*." This means that because this wind leaves the center of the heart and opens into the interior tube of the upper central channel it arises in the gateway of the path to *nirvāṇa*. If awakened awareness is transferred from the upper central channel, you attain the fruition of *nirvāṇa*. The root text continues, "When it arises downwards this is the pathway of *saṁsāra*." Since this wind opens into the central channel and moves downward inside the interior of the channel, the path of *saṁsāra* arises. If awakened awareness is transferred from the lower central channel, you remain and wander in *saṁsāra*. The root text continues, "When it arises from the right [main side channel] this is the path of faults." This refers to the white channel on the right [of the central channel], and from that all the channels on the right side [of the central channel] turn upwards. Because awakened awareness has become associated with the liveliness of the faults, consciousness-transference can occur in any of the right channels and this generates great fault. The root text continues, "When it arises from the left [main side channel], this is the path of positive qualities." This refers to the red channel on the left side [of the central channel], and from that all the channels on the left side [of the central channel] turn downwards. Because awakened awareness has become associated with the liveliness of the positive qualities, consciousness-transference can occur in any of the left channels, and this generates great benefit. The root text continues, "The three gateways [body, speech, and mind] are the path of the three realms of *saṃsāra*." This refers to the three gateways of body, speech, and mind. If consciousness-transference occurs from any of these three gateways, you will be re-born somewhere in the three realms. The root text continues, "Arising at the four gateways are the paths of the four kinds of birth." This refers to (600) the four limbs, and if consciousness-transference occurs from any of these four, you will wander among one of the four kinds of births. The root text continues, "Arising at the five gateways are the paths of the five states of being." This refers to the five gateways of the sense faculties. If consciousness-transference occurs from any of these, you are re-born in one of the five mind-stream pathways. The root text continues, "Arising at the nine gateways [orifices] are the paths of the nine levels [of practice]." This refers to the nine orifices. If consciousness-transference occurs from any of these nine orifices, you will be re-born in one or another of the nine stages.

Second, the teachings about the non-duality of the faults and positive qualities on the path are as follows: The root text says, "However, the central [channel] is the path wherein *saṃsāra* and *nirvāṇa* become non-dual." This refers to the fact that in the central channel there are no faults or positive qualities whatsoever. It is stainless. Herein, awakened awareness arises in its great original purity. The root text continues, "The king of awakened awareness arises from this path." This means that awakened awareness arises in-and-by-itself in such a way that it is straight-forward and unmistaken. If you were to ask whether it arises along any path, the root text answers by saying, "[At first, it arises from the empty expanse of the universal ground. Then, it arises as the light of the visions from the interior [of the *kati* tube channel]. Finally, it arises as realization in the central channel [and once integrated] into the mind-stream it arises from [the eye lamps]." Externally, it arises from the path of the central channel. Internally, it arises from the interior space of the five lights. Secretly, it arises straight and unmistaken from the expanse of the universal ground. If you were to ask how awakened awareness arises in whatever way on this path, the root text answers by saying, "This is the natural path of primordial, unadulterated awakened awareness." From

these three channels, as previously described, awakened awareness arises
in an unconstructed manner, in its own way. The root text says, "This
is the path of supreme primordial wisdom energy and its lucidity." This
means that awakened awareness arises not covered by obscurations. The
root text continues, "This is the unmistaken path of the energy drops."
This means that awakened awareness arises without going astray.

Third, explaining the way of consciousness-transference in the path
of the central channel has two parts: (602)

(1) The actual teaching on the way of consciousness-transference,

(2) The teachings on the benefits of consciousness-transference.

First, [the actual teaching on the way of consciousness-transference].
The root text says, "Here there is no gateway to the path of *saṁsāra*."
With respect to the central channel, it at no time can serve as the gateway to *saṁsāra*. If you were to transfer consciousness from this channel,
it is no longer possible to be re-born in *saṁsāra*. The awakened awareness
of a yogi affects the transfer of consciousness along this path. If you were
to ask how it transfers, the root text gives the answer in saying, "Awakened awareness is like the person riding the horse; and the mind—the
recollections and sense-mind—is like the horse. [Awakened awareness]
moves without any hindrances [as if riding along] by virtue of the winds.
In the central channel, the path of realization comes to completion once
coming to the secret gateway of bliss [crown *chakra*] at the crown of the
head." Here, awakened awareness is the person. The sense-mind is the
horse. The winds are the wings or the whip. The central channel is the
path. The crown chakra is the gateway. Therefore, the person of the
mind rides on the horse of the sense-mind and moves along by the whip
of the winds. Riding along the path of the central channel, consciousness-transference occurs at the crown *chakra*.

Second, the teachings on the benefits of consciousness-transference
are as follows: The root text continues, "Here, the king of awakened
awareness arises nakedly." This means that there is no occasion for afflictive emotions and conceptual thought to move in the path of the central channel. When consciousness-transference occurs from that gateway
[at the crown *chakra*], awakened awareness arises without obscuration or

covering, bare and naked. The root text continues, "and the layer of conceptual thought is stripped off." This means that self-purification occurs without having to abandon afflictive emotions or conceptual thought [using a remedy]. For example, it is like a person who is not wearing any clothes and is naked. The root text then says, "Here is where the face of self-occurring primordial wisdom is seen." This means that it is not necessary to be taught by a master because awakened awareness recognizes its own face in-and-by-itself. The text continues, "Here, the darkness of non-awakened awareness and delusion is purified." (603) This means that because awakened awareness is self-arising, the darkness is purified in-and-by-itself.

The root text says, "Here the gateways to the three realms [of *saṃsāra*] and the nine levels [of practice] are stirred up." This passage means that because the three gateways of body, speech, and mind have been obstructed, the three realms have been stirred from their depths. Because the nine orifices have become obstructed, the nine levels have been stirred from their depths. The root text continues, "and the path of the five poisons and afflictive emotions is cut off." Because the five gateways of the sense organs have been obstructed, the continuum of the five poisons is cut off. The root text continues, "Here the ocean of *saṃsāra* and the six types of beings dries up." This means that because the causes [of *saṃsāra*] have been eradicated, the consequences, namely the six types of beings [and the six realms of *saṃsāra*] dry up. The root text continues, "Here the gateways to the four kinds of births within *saṃsāra* are emptied out." This means that because the gateways of the four limbs have been blocked, the four kinds of births have been eradicated. The root text finishes by saying, "Here the three-fold embodiment of enlightenment arises in-and-by-itself continuously." This means that since the three-fold embodiment of enlightenment has arisen in-and-by-itself and keeps arising over and over, they [enlightened bodies] come to serve the benefit of all beings [inexhaustibly].

Third, the conclusion is clearly expressed in the root text by saying, "This completes the nail of the straight unmistaken path. (604) *Samaya!*"

11: The Nail of Dispelling the Delusion of Non-Awakened Awareness, the Lamp for Dispelling Darkness

Homage to Kun tu bZang po, who dispels the delusion of not recognizing awakened awareness. Primordial wisdom's self-awakened awareness arises in the five gateways. With respect to the five sense-objects, they are clear when there is not yet conceptual thought [about these objects]. With respect to these sense-objects, the mind-consciousness [generates] conceptual thought [about them].

The path for seeing awakened awareness is through the gateway of the [fluid eye] lamps. By means of the extensive lasso of the fluid eye lamp, the thickened darkness of the seeming ordinary world of appearance becomes purified. By means of the lamp of the visions and special insight into these, the darkness of useless conceptual thought becomes purified. By means of the lamp of primordial wisdom's self-awakened awareness, the darkness of not recognizing awakened awareness through conceptualizing is purified. By means of the lamp of the expanse of the universal ground, the darkness of partial, limited, or biased thinking is purified.

The king of awakened awareness arises in this [mode of non-conceptual] seeing. It arises in the empty space of the universal ground. The visions arise in the light of the interior [of the *kati* tube lamp]. The lucidity of everything arises in the gateway of the [eye] lamp. Just like a lotus that arises from the mud, the king of awakened awareness comes from the interior [of the *kati* tube channel]. Just like the sun devoid of all darkness, the king of awakened awareness is free of the darkness of obscuration. The six divine eyes arise from the forehead. These [divine] eyes see [everything] nakedly, and the enlightened intention [of Kun tu bZang po] is thoroughly complete. This completes the nail of the lamp for dispelling darkness. *Samaya!*

Eleventh, the nail of the lamp that dispels the darkness has three parts. The first part expresses the homage when the root text says, "Homage to Kun tu bZang po, who dispels the delusion of non-awakened awareness." This means that, with respect to *bodhicitta*, it cannot be obscured by darkness or covered [by anything].

Second, the extensive explanation has three parts:

(1) Explaining how the five gateways [of the senses] are used on the path for seeing awakened awareness,

(2) Specifically, explaining the path for seeing awakened awareness through the eye lamp, and

(3) Explaining the arising of primordial wisdom's awakened awareness in the gateway of the eye lamp and the thorough completion that ensues.

First, [explaining how the five gateways [of the senses] are used on the path for seeing awakened awareness] begins with the root text, "Primordial wisdom's self-awakened awareness arises in the five gateways." This passage refers to the king of awakened awareness, the essence (604) of the great single unified sphere of ultimate reality. From the liveliness of the five lights and the five elements, awakened awareness arises in the five gateways of the sense-faculties. The root text continues, "With respect to the five sense-objects, they are clear when there is no conceptual thought [about these objects]." This means that with respect to the five gateways of the sense faculties, the king of awakened awareness arises free of thought much like a clean mirror. The play of the seeming five external sense-objects arises like reflections in a mirror. Even though they arise, the king of awakened awareness is free of even the smallest particle of conceptual thought grasping at an object. If you were to ask how any kind of conceptual thought [grasps after the sense] object, the root text answers when it says, "With respect to these sense-objects, the mind-consciousness [generates] conceptual thought [about them]." This means that [the entire] magical display of the mind is thought up by the mental consciousness.

Second, specifically, explaining the path for seeing awakened awareness through the eye lamp is as follows: The root text begins, "The path for seeing awakened awareness is the gateway of the [fluid eye] lamps." This passage explains that the gateways of the eye [lamps] are the foundation for awakened awareness arising in-and-by-itself. Because all four lamps can be said to arise in each of these [eye lamp] gateways, this affects the dispelling of the four kinds of darkness.

As the root text continues, "By means of the extensive lasso of the fluid eye lamp, the thickened darkness of the seeming ordinary world of appearance becomes purified." This means that if the fluid eye lamps did not exist, you would be thoroughly immersed in the darkness of the seeming external world. However, because the fluid eye lamp exists, you are freed from all the darkness of this seeming external world.

The root text continues, "By means of the lamp of the visions and special insight into these, the darkness of useless conceptual thought becomes purified."

This means that if there were no special insight into seeing the three visions—ultimate sound, light, and light-rays—then the mind would remain immersed in the darkness of nihilism. However, because the visions of these three—ultimate sound, light, and light-rays—have arisen [in the context of special insight], then seeing is free of the darkness of the view of empty nihilism.

The root text continues, "By means of the lamp of primordial wisdom's self-awakened awareness, the darkness of not recognizing awakened awareness through conceptualizing is purified." This means that if there were no lamp of co-emergent awakened awareness, (605) then [the mind] would remain immersed in the darkness of non-recognition of awakening and conceptual thought. However, because there has been recognition of co-emergent awakened awareness, then the darkness of non-recognition of awakening is dispelled in-and-by-itself.

The root text continues, "By means of the lamp of the expanse of the universal ground, the darkness of partial, limited, or biased thinking is purified." This means that if there were no realization of the limitless expanse of the universal ground, then [the mind] would remain immersed in the darkness of grasping after different schools of thought, partialities or divisions. However, if there has been realization of the universal ground, then this truth will not deviate into eternalism, nihilism, or any other partialities whatsoever, and all the darkness of schools of thought and extreme views become liberated in-and-by-themselves.

In this way, these four lamps all arise in-and-by-themselves continuously in the gateways of the eye lamps. If you realize the ultimate truth of this, not even the name of that darkness that brings obscuration can exist.

Third, explaining the arising of primordial wisdom's awakened awareness in the gateway of the eye lamp and the thorough completion that ensues is as follows: The root text begins, "The king of awakened awareness arises in this [mode of non-conceptual] seeing." This passage refers to primordial wisdom arising in-and-by-itself. If you were to ask, where do you see whatever arises arising, the root text answers in saying, "It arises in the empty space of the universal ground. The visions arise in the light of the interior [of the *kati* tube lamp]. The lucidity of everything arises in the gateway of the [eye] lamp." This means that externally, it arises in the gateways of the eye lamps. Internally, it arises in seeing the five lights. Secretly, it arises in seeing the universal ground. If you were to ask how it arises in any way, the root text explains by saying, "Just like a lotus that arises from the mud, the king of awakened awareness comes from the interior [of the *kati* tube channel]." For example, a lotus is born within mud. Yet [once it blossoms] it remains nakedly, untouched by the mud. Similarly, with respect to awakened awareness, in the gateways of the eye [lamps], the illusions [of the ordinary world] come out of the interior of the [*kati* tube channel] in the body. The visions come out of the interior of the [channels] in the sense-objects. (606) Conceptual thought comes out of the interior of the [channels] of conceptual thought. Each of these respectively arises naked and bare, without being stained by anything whatsoever. The root text continues, "Just like the sun devoid of all darkness, the king of awakened awareness is free of the darkness of obscuration." With respect to the sun that is free of darkness, no obscurations whatsoever exist, and likewise, in the gateways of the eye lamps, the king of awakened awareness arises bare, free from the darkness and obscurations of the body. It is also free from the darkness and obscurations of sense-objects. It is also free of the darkness and obscurations of conceptual thought. It arises vividly and lucidly without any obscurations and coverings.

The root text continues, "The six divine eyes arise continuously from the forehead." This means that in the gateways of the eye lamps, the six divine eyes arise in-and-by-themselves in a continuous manner. Furthermore, these six divine eyes are explained as follows:

(1) Because awakened awareness arises without obscuration, this is the divine eye of primordial wisdom,

(2) Because it arises without confusion, this is the divine eye of awakened awareness,

(3) Because it arises unobstructedly, this is the divine eye of compassion,

(4) Because it arises without representation, this is the divine eye of knowledge,

(5) Because it arises unmixed, this is the divine eye of emanation,

(6) Because it arises unconstructed, this is the divine eye of awakened mind-itself.

The root text continues, "These [divine] eyes see [everything] nakedly, and the enlightened intention [of Kun tu bZang po] is thoroughly complete." In this way, in the gateways of the eye lamps, the six divine eyes arise continuously in-and-by-themselves, and if the realization of each of these is bare and naked, then the ultimate truth of the natural state and the enlightened intentions of *Buddhahood* are completed, without remainder.

Third, the conclusion is clearly explained when the root text says, "This completes the nail of the lamp for dispelling darkness. *Samaya!*"

12: The Nail of Beyond Being United With or Separated From the Three-fold Embodiment of Enlightenment, Pointing Out the Three Essential Points

Homage to Kun tu bZang po, who is beyond [ever] being united with or being separated from the three-fold embodiment of enlightenment. Primordial wisdom's self-awakened awareness is the original purity of the *dharmakāya*. Connecting body and mind is the Completion Body [*sambhogakāya*]. The various specific [emanations] that arise are the Emanation Bodies [*nirmānakāyas*]. Because awakened awareness has arisen from within the depths of the universal ground, its essence is beyond [ever] being united with or separated [from anything whatsoever]. Through the liveliness of awakened awareness, and through its [complete] purification, there is no way to go astray on this path. (559) Because the fruition arises in the gateways, the three-fold embodiment of enlightenment [that arises] is not covered by obscuration. The self-awakened awareness that arises from within the domain of the physical heart is the *dharmakāya*. In the path of the [*kati*] channel, its real nature is the *sambhogakāya*. In the gateways of the [fluid eye] lamps are the self-arising *nirmāṇakāyas*.

From within the depths, self-arisen [awakened awareness] stays as primordial *Buddhahood*. Within the interior [of the *kati* tube channel], it arises as spontaneously present *Buddhahood* in its completion. With respect to seeing [the visions], without obscuration, this seeing arises as fully manifested *Buddhahood*. Through realizing the universal ground, there is meeting with the mother, the natural state. Because heretofore hidden or concealed primordial wisdom has been revealed, all the darkness that covers and obscures is purified. Because naked awakened awareness overflows, the three-fold embodiment of enlightenment becomes directly evident. Through realization about the conditions [that support] delusion, a thorough determination has been made about delusion. Through the finger-pointing [instructions] about the natural state, both doubt and the ordinary sense-mind are exhausted. Through opening the door to the treasury of awakened awareness, the treasury of the universal ground is completely penetrated. This completes the nail of pointing out the three essential points. *Samaya!*

Twelfth, the nail of pointing out the three essential points has three parts.

First, the root text gives the homage in saying, "Homage to Kun tu bZang po, who is beyond [ever] being united with or being separated from the three-fold embodiment of enlightenment. Primordial wisdom's self-awakened awareness is the original purity of the *dharmakāya*." (607) This explains the homage. This means that *bodhicitta* arises in-and-by-itself as the three-fold embodiment of enlightenment.

Second, the extensive explanation has five parts:

(1) Pointing out the three-fold embodiment of enlightenment, which

stays in its own way,

(2) Pointing out the three—basis, path, and fruition—which stay in their own way,

(3) With respect to the three bases, pointing out how the three enlightened bodies arise in-and-by-themselves,

(4) With respect to the three bases, pointing out these as *Buddhahood*,

(5) Explaining the significance of these instructions.

First, pointing out the three-fold embodiment of enlightenment, which stays in its own way, is as follows: The root text begins, "Primordial wisdom's self-awakened awareness is the original purity of the *dharmakāya*." This means that primordial wisdom's self-awakened awareness is untouched by any limitations whatsoever. Because the *dharmakāya*] arises in-and-by-itself, this *dharmakāya* stays in its own way.

The root text continues, "Connecting body and mind is the Completion Body [*sambhogakāya*]." This refers to the body and mind being unified as a pair. As such, the five elements, five poisons, etc. (i.e. all the phenomena of *saṃsāra*), and the five enlightened *Buddha* bodies, the five families, the five wisdoms, etc. (i.e. all the phenomena of *nirvāṇa*), whether they are or are not adequately realized by anyone, because they are thoroughly completed without remainder, the enlightened Completion Body [*sambhogakāya*] stays in its own way.

The root text continues, "The various particulars that arise are the Emanation Bodies [*nirmāṇakāyas*]." This means that from the liveliness of connecting the body and mind as a pair, the various activities of the three gates [body, speech, and mind] arise. Whether these are adequately realized or not realized, since this magical display of the mind arises in-and-by-itself, the enlightened Emanation Bodies [*nirmāṇakāyas*] stay in their own way.

Second, pointing out the three—basis, path, and fruition—that stay in their own way is as follows: The root text begins, "Because awakened awareness has arisen from within the depths of the universal ground, its essence is beyond [ever] being united with or separated [from anything whatsoever]." This means that the basis of awakened awareness is its heart-essence. If the ultimate truth of this is realized (608) you will never be separated from the ultimate truth of the natural state. The root text continues, "Through the liveliness of awakened awareness and its [complete] purification, there is no way to go astray on this path." This explains that the path of awakened awareness is the central channel. If this pathway of the central channel is purified, the text explains that this is the path to *Buddhahood* without going astray. The root text continues, "Because the fruition arises in the gateways, the three-fold embodiment of enlightenment [that arises] is not covered by obscuration." This means that the fruition of the three-fold embodiment of enlightenment arises in-and-by-itself in the gateways of the eye lamps. If the ultimate truth of this is realized, then the three-fold embodiment of enlightenment becomes directly evident without obscuration or covering.

Third, with respect to the three bases, pointing out how the three enlightened bodies arise in-and-by-themselves is as follows: The root text begins, "Self-awakened awareness that arises from within the domain of the physical heart is *dharmakāya*." This means that because awakened awareness stays and arises in-and-by-itself in the heart, it also means that the *dharmakāya* arises in-and-by-itself. The root text continues, "In the path of the [*kati*] channel, its real nature is the *sambhogakāya*." This means that the liveliness of awakened awareness is thoroughly complete in the central channel. This also means that the enlightened Completion Body arises in-and-by-itself. The root text continues, "In the gateways of the [eye] lamps are the self-arising Emanation Bodies [*nirmāṇakāyas*]." This means that all the magical displays of the mind, without exception, arise in the gateways of the eye lamps. It also means that the enlightened Emanation Bodies [*nirmāṇakāyas*] arise in-and-by-themselves.

Fourth, with respect to the three bases, pointing out these as *Buddhahood* is as follows: The root text says, "From within the depths, self-arisen [awakened awareness] stays as primordial *Buddhahood*." This means that *Buddhahood* is the primordial *Buddhahood* that stays within the depths of the heart. The root text continues, "Within the interior [of the *kati* tube channel] it arises as spontaneously present *Buddhahood* in its completion." This means that *Buddhahood* is the mind that stays as completion *Buddhahood* in the interior of the *kati* channel. The root text continues, "With respect to seeing [the visions], without obscuration, this seeing arises as

fully manifested *Buddhahood*." (609) This means that in the gateways of
the eye lamps, the mind arises as fully manifesting *Buddhahood*.

Fifth, explaining the significance of these instructions is as follows:
The root text begins, "Through realizing the universal ground, there is
meeting with the mother, the natural state." This means that since no
other natural state exists beyond the universal ground, such a realization
comes from these instructions, so that the mother and son meet, which
is awakened mind-itself. The root text continues, "Because heretofore
hidden or concealed primordial wisdom has been revealed, all the darkness that covers and obscures is purified." This means that through this
instruction, this heretofore hidden primordial wisdom is revealed in the
gateways of the eye lamps. Since everything is shown without obscuration or covering, there is no longer obscuration by any kind of darkness
whatsoever. The root text continues, "Because naked awakened awareness overflows, the three-fold embodiment of enlightenment becomes
directly evident." This means that since naked awakened awareness was
directly pointed out in the gateways of the eye lamps, the three-fold embodiment of enlightenment directly becomes evident.

The root text continues, "Through realization about the conditions
[that support] delusion, a thorough determination has been made about
delusion." This means that since the three—ultimate sound, light, and
light-rays—are realized to be [possible] conditions for delusion, and since
there has been decisive determination about delusion, then delusion no
longer exists. The root text continues, "Through the finger-pointing [in-
structions] about the natural state, both doubt and the ordinary sense-
mind are exhausted." This means that through these instructions a decisive determination has been made about the natural state, and thus as it
was shown through finger-pointing, then it is explained that there can be
no doubt left in the mind.

The root text says, "Through opening the door to the treasury of
awakened awareness, the treasury of the universal ground is completely
penetrated." Externally, this means that since one has opened the door
of this treasury of instructions, the treasury of *dharmakāya* has been penetrated. Internally, since one has opened the door of the treasury of the
eye lamps, the treasury of the three visions—ultimate sound, light, and
light-rays—has been penetrated. Secretly, since one has opened the door

of awakened awareness, the treasury of the universal ground has been penetrated.

Third, (610) the conclusion is clearly explained in the text when it says, "This completes the nail of pointing out the three essential points. *Samaya!*"

13: The Nail of Self-Awakened Awareness, the Root Deity, Pointing Out the *Mandala*

Homage to Kun tu bZang po, whose self-awakened awareness is the root deity. The display of the spontaneously present *mandala* and its *mudras* is within the domain of space of the universal ground, which is emptiness/clarity, which is the expanse of *dharmadhātu*. The thumb-sized primordial awareness [that arises in the heart lamp] is the self-occurring *dharmakāya*. The three—sound, light, and light-rays—are the arising activities of the *sambhogakāya*. The three types of magical displays that self-occur are the *nirmānakāyas*. The five appearing [wisdom] lights are the basis for the pure realms and the [sacred] *mandala*. The five energy drops, like an offering tent, become the immeasurable palaces for the five [*Buddha*] families. With respect to the enlightened embodiment of special insight, various enlightened form bodies arise. The three-fold unification [of the three gateways—body, speech, and mind] becomes the basis of emanation of the three-fold embodiment of enlightenment. These also arise as the five deities, the five [*Buddha*] families and the five wisdoms, the five male and female deities and their retinues, (560) inconceivable [in number]. The real nature of this great *mandala* is not created through effort. With respect to *bodhicitta*, the *mandala* of the three-fold embodiment of enlightenment is complete. Because this *mandala* arises-in-and-by-itself, it is not accomplished through any effort. Because these visions are without any real nature, there is neither attachment nor aversion to them. This completes the nail of pointing out the *mandala*. *Samaya!*

Thirteenth, the nail of pointing out the *mandala* has three parts, the first of which is the homage. The root text says, "Homage to Kun tu bZang po, whose awakened awareness-itself is the root deity." This explains the homage. This refers to the basis of arising of *bodhicitta* [expressed as] the outer, inner, and secret *mandalas*, and as the assemblies of deities who are pacifying, causing flourishing, influencing, and using intense means.

Second, the extensive explanation begins, "The display of the spontaneously present *mandala* and its *mudras* is...." This passage means that with respect to *bodhicitta*, it is not necessary to visualize the *mandalas* of the deities of *Mahamudrā* because they are explained as being complete in their own way. If you were to ask how they are complete, the root text answers by saying, "The domain of space of the universal ground, which is emptiness/clarity, is the expanse of the *dharmadhātu*." This means that in the expanse of the universal ground the celestial palaces and pure realms of the *dharmakāya* are revealed.

The root text continues, "The thumb-sized primordial awareness [that arises in the heart lamp] is the self-occurring *dharmakāya*." This means that primordial wisdom's awakened awareness is explained as the essence of the *dharmakāya*. The root text continues, "The three—sound, light, and light-rays—are the arising activities of the *sambhogakāya*." This means that these three great visions are explained as the essence of the Completion Body [*sambhogakāya*]. The root text continues, "The three types of magical displays that self-occur are the *nirmāṇakāyas*." This means that from the liveliness of connecting the three great visions and awakened awareness, the magical displays of ordinary body, speech, and mind arise as the displays of enlightened body, speech, and mind. These are explained as the essence of the Emanation Bodies [*nirmāṇakāyas*].

The root text continues, "The five appearing [wisdom] lights are the basis for the pure realms and the [sacred] *mandala*." This means that the five kinds of [wisdom] lights are explained as the basis of arising of the pure realms of the Completion Body and the Emanation Bodies. (611) The root text continues, "The five energy drops, like an offering tent, become the immeasurable palaces for the five [*Buddha*] families." This means that the energy drops of the offering tent of the five lights and the energy drops of awakened awareness that are crystal-like are explained to be the basis of arising of the celestial palaces of the five *Bud-*

dha families. The root text continues, "With respect to the enlightened embodiment of special insight, various enlightened form bodies arise." It means that these reflections of the enlightened embodiment of special insight are explained to be the basis of arising of the various Completion and Emanation Bodies. The root text continues, "The three-fold unification becomes the basis of emanation of the three-fold embodiment of enlightenment." This means that the connection of these [five] lights with awakened awareness becomes the basis of the emanation of the enlightened body; the connection of ultimate sound with awakened awareness becomes the basis of the emanation of all the ways of enlightened speech; and the connection of light-rays with awakened awareness becomes the basis of connection of the emanation of all the ways of enlightened mind. The root text continues, "These also arise as the five deities, the five [*Buddha*] families and the five wisdoms, the five male and female deities and their retinues, inconceivable [in number]." This means that the connection to and unification of the three visions and awakened awareness is the basis of arising of inconceivable numbers of emanations. The root text continues, "The real nature of this great *mandala* is not created through effort." This means that the *mandalas* of the deities of *Mahamudrā* arise in the mind but are not brought about through any effort, as in the lower vehicles. This great *mandala* by nature arises as spontaneously present. The root text continues, "With respect to *bodhicitta*, the *mandala* of the three-fold embodiment of enlightenment is complete." This means that from the very beginning these [*mandalas*] arise in-and-by-themselves as clear. The root text continues, "Because this *mandala* arises-in-itself, it is not created through any effort." This means that since the *mandalas* of the three enlightened *Buddha* bodies arise in one's own mind as primordially present, it is not necessary to develop them or search for them, as in the lower vehicles. (612) The root text says, "Because these visions are without any real nature, do not have attachment or aversion to them." This means that the *mandalas* of the three-fold embodiment of enlightenment appear in the mind as spontaneously present and therefore, like the eight metaphors about illusion, since they lack inherent nature, there is crossing over to where no attachment whatsoever can exist.

Third, the conclusion is clearly explained in the root text when it says, "This completes the nail of pointing out the mandala. *Samaya!*"

14: The Nail of the Enlightened Body that is the Self-Occurring Single Interconnected Sphere

Homage to Kun tu bZang po, who is the enlightened body, the self-occurring single interconnected sphere [of ultimate reality]. The essence of mind is the [awakened] mind-itself. Space is the inherent radiance of the mind. The final realization of mind is the *dharmadhātu*. [This space-like mind] pervades everything without outside or inside. The full measure of the visions is the play of the enlightened body. The full measure of speech is the play of enlightened speech. The full measure of the mind is the play of the enlightened heart-mind. The full measure of the elements is the play of the [enlightened] positive qualities. The full measure of doing is the play of enlightened activity. They are all complete within this single [great] interconnected sphere [of ultimate reality]. This completes the nail for pointing out the single interconnected sphere [of ultimate reality]. *Samaya!*

Fourteenth, the nail that points out the single, interconnected sphere, has three parts, the first of which explains the homage in the root text as follows: "Homage to Kun tu bZang po, who is the enlightened body, the self-occurring single interconnected sphere [of ultimate reality]." This passage is explained in terms of *bodhicitta* and the single, interconnected sphere as being inseparable.

Second, the extensive explanation has two parts:

(1) The awakened mind-itself shown to be the ultimate truth of the single, interconnected sphere, and

(2) All the visions that are beyond being external and internal are shown to be the liveliness and play of that.

First, the awakened mind-itself shown to be the ultimate truth of the single, interconnected sphere is as follows: The root text begins, "The essence of mind is [awakened] mind-itself. Space is the inherent radiance of the mind. The final realization of mind is *dharmadhātu*." This means that the essence of *bodhicitta* is inherent awakened awareness that arises in-and-of-itself. Thus, it is given the name "awakened mind-itself." Thus, it is given the name "space." The natural state that signifies reaching the end of the path of the mind stays without sound, reflections, or words. Thus, it is given the name "*dharmakāya*." The root text continues, "[This space-like mind] pervades everything without outside or inside." This means that at the time *bodhicitta* (613) pervades the elements externally, it is called "space." When it pervades the sense-faculties internally, it is called "awakened mind-itself." When it stays pervading and encompassing everything without outside or inside, it is called *dharmadhātu*. In a similar manner, the three—examples, meaning, and signs—are affixed to this single, interconnected sphere [of ultimate reality]. With respect to ultimate truth, these remain as inseparable from each other.

Second, all the visions that are beyond being external and internal are shown to be the liveliness and play of that as follows: The root text begins, "The full measure of the visions is the play of the enlightened body. The full measure of speech is the play of enlightened speech. The full measure of mind is the play of the enlightened heart-mind. The full measure of the elements is the play of the [enlightened] positive qualities. The full measure of doing is the play of enlightened activity." This means that although all of these—the full measure of the visions, the full measure of speech, the full measure of the mind, the full measure of the elements, and the full measure of doing—occur, they occur as a result of *bodhicitta*. Although they stay, they stay in that [*bodhicitta*]. Although they become liberated, they become liberated in that [*bodhicitta*]. What is to be known is that this is not [ordinary] mind. There is not even the smallest particle of this [ordinary mind]. What is to be known is that everything is the play of [awakened] mind that arises in-and-by-itself. The root text says, "They are all complete within this single [great] interconnected sphere [of ultimate reality]."

This means that within awakened mind-itself, within this single, interconnected sphere, of all the phenomena of *saṃsāra* and *nirvāṇa*, nothing is not complete, and thus, everything is completed as the same taste in this [awakened] mind.

Third, the conclusion is clearly explained in the root text when it says, "This completes the nail for pointing out the single interconnected sphere. *Samaya!*"

15: The Nail of Being Without the Obscuration of Karmic Propensities, Making the Determination of Mother and Son

Homage to Kun tu bZang po, who is without the obscuration of karmic propensities. After making a close-to-the-heart determination of the karmic propensities within the universal ground, investigate further to untie the knot of [any] attachment. Because this cuts to the root of karmic seeds, it is said there is no turning back [to *samsāra*]. Emptiness and clarity are the universal basis, like space. The elements and the seemingly existing world are liveliness. Yet, chasing after them is how delusion [develops]. [Yet], viewing this as a fault is to go astray. The [best] skillful means is [to keep the mind] relaxed and let things go their own way. This is the path to liberation, [where everything is immediately liberated] in the domain of the space [of the universal ground]. When the realization is free of [any] duality, the fruition directly manifests itself.

Primordial wisdom is effortless in the [universal] ground. The various activities [within the universal ground] are its liveliness. Yet, chasing after them is how delusion [develops]. [Yet], viewing this as a fault is to go astray. (561) The [best] skillful means is [to keep the mind] relaxed and let things go their own way. This is the path of liberation in the domain of space. When realization is free of [any] duality, the fruition directly manifests itself.

Primordial wisdom is expressionless in the [universal] ground. The various expressions are its liveliness. Yet, chasing after them is how delusion [develops]. [Yet], viewing this as a fault is to go astray. The [best] skillful means is [to keep the mind] relaxed and let things go their own way. This is the path of liberation in the domain of space. When realization is free of [any] duality, the fruition directly manifests itself.

Primordial wisdom is free of conceptual thought in the [universal] ground. The various recollections and conceptual thoughts are its liveliness. Yet, chasing after them is how delusion [develops]. [Yet], viewing this as a fault is to go astray. The [best] skillful means is [to keep the mind] relaxed and let things go their own way. This is the path of liberation in the domain of space. When realization is free of [any] duality, the fruition directly manifests itself.

Primordial wisdom is self-occurring in the [universal] ground. The afflictive emotions and five poisons are its liveliness. Yet, chasing after these visions is how delusion [develops]. [Yet], viewing this as a fault is to go astray. The [best] skillful means is [to keep the mind] relaxed and let things go their own way. This is the path of liberation in the domain of space. When realization is free of [any] duality, the fruition directly manifests itself.

Primordial wisdom is self-awakened awareness in the [universal] ground. The three—ultimate sound, light, and light-rays—are its liveliness. Yet, grasping them as real [and independently existing] is how delusion [develops]. [Yet], viewing this as superior is to go astray. The [best] skillful means is make a close-to-the-heart determination. This is the path of liberation in the domain of space. Realizing [everything] being without real nature, the fruition arises as liveliness. This completes the nail of making a close-to-the-heart determination about mother and son. *Samaya!*

Fifteenth, the nail of making a close-to-the-heart determination of mother and son, has three parts, the first of which is the homage as explained in the root text, "Homage to Kun tu bZang po, who is without the obscuration of karmic propensities." This passage explains the meaning of the homage. This means that *bodhicitta* is completely pure without any kind of [karmic] attachments. (614)

Second, the extensive explanation has two parts—a brief and a more detailed explanation.

First is the brief explanation. The root text begins, "After a close-to-the-heart determination of karmic propensities in the universal ground...." This means that if the mind-stream of an individual is interrupted [by death], the seeds of habitual karmic propensities and af-

flictive emotions become manifest in both respects. However, because
of taking up the practice of this path, there is liberation from the direct
manifestation of these [karmic propensities and] afflictive emotions. If
there is no decisive determination about the cause [of manifestation],
which are the seeds of habitual karmic propensities [ripening], then it is
still possible to produce afflictive emotions at this current moment from
the [ripening] causes of habitual karmic propensities. Therefore, it is
said that it is necessary to make a decisive determination about these
seeds of habitual karmic propensities. If you were to ask how [the ripening of these karmic propensities] can be stopped, the root text answers,
"Investigate further to untie the knot of [any] attachment." Making an
accumulation of habitual karmic propensities as an overlay on the universal ground is a kind of grasping. Acting in a manner that does not
let them go is to be attached to them. Being tied up by the ropes of
grasping, and restrained by the knots of attachment, you are not able to
let go of habitual karmic propensities. For example, this is like accumu-
lating wealth by someone who clings to it. Regarding that, an individual
who is on this path takes up the meditation practice without clinging to
or grasping anything whatsoever, such that these habitual karmic propensities become purified in-and-by-themselves. For example, it is like a
[cache of] jewels without an owner. The root text continues, "Because
this cuts to the root of karmic seeds, it is said there is no turning back [to
saṃsāra]." For example, if you extinguish a fire in the hearth, the effect is
to cut down smoke on the walls. Because there has been a decisive determination about the cause, namely the seeds of habitual karmic propensities [ripening], the [overall] effect thereafter is that afflictive emotions
can never again develop. Thus, it is said that one will never again revert
back to remaining in *saṃsāra* thereafter. (615)

Second, is the more detailed explanation. Six skillful means of meditation practice of the path are explained and each of them has eight
parts:

(1) the six bases,

(2) the six livelinesses,

(3) the six ways of becoming deluded,

(4) the six ways of going astray,

(5) the six skillful means,

(6) the six paths,

(7) the six realizations, and

(8) the six fruitions. These are explained as follows:

Regarding the six bases,

(1) *Bodhicitta* stays as all-pervasive and all-encompassing, empty and clear. It stays as the basis of arising of the elements and also of all phenomenal existence.

(2) This stays free of action, yet is the basis of arising of all the various actions.

(3) It stays without expression, yet is the basis of arising of all the variety of expressions.

(4) It stays free of conceptual thought, yet is the basis of arising of the great variety of recollections and conceptual thoughts.

(5) It stays as self-occurring primordial wisdom, and yet is the basis of arising of the afflictive emotions and five poisons.

(6) It stays as primordial wisdom's inherent awakened awareness, yet is the basis of arising of the three visions—ultimate sound, light, and light-rays—yet, even though these six bases are explained as such, they are manifestations of *bodhicitta*.

Second, regarding the six livelinesses:

(1) The elements of the seeming existing world are the liveliness of space.

(2) The various kinds of actions are the liveliness that is without action.

(3) The various different kinds of expressions are the liveliness that is without expression.

(4) The various different kinds of recollections and conceptual thoughts are the liveliness that is free of thought.

(5) The afflictive emotions and the five poisons are the liveliness of self-occurring primordial wisdom.

(6) The three—ultimate sound, light, and light-rays—are the liveliness of awakened awareness. Although these six livelinesses are explained in this way, they are the inherent liveliness of *bodhicitta*.

Third, regarding the six ways of becoming deluded. Because of chasing after the six types of liveliness, one wanders in *saṃsāra*.

Fourth, the six ways of going astray: From viewing [chasing after] the six livelinesses as a fault, one abandons this. From viewing these however as superior, you come to view these as absolutely good and thereby go astray. (616)

Fifth, the six skillful means: Not viewing the six livelinesses as a fault or grasping them as superior, by not chasing after them, ones eases up and lets them go their own way, and in this way liberation from *saṃsāra* comes from liberation in-and-by-itself.

Sixth, the six paths: Therefore, by easing up and letting the six livelinesses go their own way, by practicing meditation in this way, they become liberated in their own way in the domain of space of the six bases. For example, it is like the clouds [clearing] from the sky, or like [mud] stirred up in water [settling down].

Seventh, the six realizations: From purifying the six livelinesses in-and-by-themselves in the domain of space of the six bases, there is the realization that the mind as mother and son are inseparable.

Eighth, the six fruitions: From having purified the habitual karmic propensities of the six livelinesses in their own way, the natural state of the six bases directly manifests itself. *Samādhi* and post-*samādhi* become inseparable and directly manifest [as one continuous state].

Third, the root text clearly explains the conclusion in saying, "This completes the nail of making a close-to-the-heart determination about mother and son. *Samaya!*"

16: The Nail of Non-Localization, Going Beyond, Crossing Over

Homage to Kun tu bZang po, who is not localized and goes beyond [everything]. In the expanse of the universal ground, nothing falls into partiality. Primordial wisdom's awakened awareness is without eyes and beyond [all] expressions. With respect to recollections and ideas [in the universal ground], they are insubstantial yet unobstructed [in their expression]. **Do not have attachment or aversion to the three—ultimate sound, light, and light-rays. (562) Do not grasp them as conditioned/unconditioned, or as inferior/superior. Do not view them as purity or dregs, or as of benefit or fault. *Samsāra* and *nirvāna* remain inseparable, and cannot be divided. *Buddhas* and sentient beings are inseparable, and are not different. There is neither entrance into nor travelling along the path of awakened awareness. *Bodhicitta* is beyond [the differences of] schools of thought or vehicles. Everything remains as sameness, without [distinctions like] good or bad, higher or lower. This completes the nail of crossing over into sameness. *Samaya!***

Sixteenth, the nail of crossing over into sameness has three parts, the first of which is the homage, and the root text says, "Homage to Kun tu bZang po, who is not localized and goes beyond [everything]." This expresses the meaning of the homage. This means that *bodhicitta* does not abide anywhere in any limits throughout *samsāra* and *nirvāna*, and is said to go beyond everything as *nirvāna*.

Second, the extensive meaning is as follows: The root text begins, "In the expanse of the universal ground nothing falls into partiality." This means that the natural state of the universal ground (617) crosses over, in that it does not fall into the extremes of eternalism and nihilism, nor does it fall into any [other] partialities. The root text continues, "Primordial wisdom's awakened awareness is without eyes and beyond expression." This means that the natural state of awakened awareness crosses over in that it is beyond the action of conceptual thought and beyond expression in words. The root text continues, "With respect to recollections and ideas [in the universal ground], they are insubstantial yet unobstructed [in their expression]." This means that the natural state of conceptual thought, by virtue of being without a basis or root, is impermanent. However, since [thought activity] is unobstructed, there is nothing to cut off. It crosses over in that [thought] is beyond arising and ceasing. The root text continues, "Do not have attachment or aversion for the three—ultimate sound, light, and light-rays." This means that since these three great visions are self-arising [expressions] of

mind, there is neither attachment nor aversion to them. It crosses over
in that one is beyond attachment to them. The root text continues, "Do
not grasp them as conditioned/unconditioned, or as inferior/superior."
This means that although the ordinary aggregates have karmic outflows,
and the lights, energy drops, divine bodies and their celestial palaces do
not have karmic outflows, since they are the same taste as *bodhicitta*, they
are not grasped as having karmic outflows and being inferior, or as not
having karmic outflows and being superior. It crosses over in that it is
beyond such dualities. The root text continues, "Do not view them as
purity or dregs, or as of benefit or fault." This means that the five lights
that are radiant elemental energies and the five elements that are impure dregs—fire, water, earth, wind, and space, and also the flesh, blood,
warmth, and breath that come alive from the five elements—since they
all have the same taste with respect to *bodhicitta*, they are respectively not
seen as beneficial, radiant, elemental energies, nor as faulty elements
that are impure dregs. This is crossing over as sameness. The root text
continues, "*Saṁsāra* and *nirvāṇa* remain inseparable, and cannot be divided." This means that even though the phenomena of *saṁsāra* and the
phenomena of *nirvāṇa* are two, since nothing exists as to the manner of
grasping at these with the conceptual mind, (618) then, as these share the
same taste as the magical display of the mind, it is crossing over in that
there is no distinguishing each of these as a duality. The root text continues, "*Buddhas* and sentient beings are inseparable and are not different."
This means that although *Buddhas* and sentient beings are two with respect to having or not having realization, there is no difference. In their
essence there is no distinction such as good or bad. This is crossing over
in that, with respect to state of mind, there is no difference. The root text
continues, "There is neither entrance into nor travelling along the path
of awakened awareness." This means that the path of *bodhicitta* is free of
any need to travel on it, because one is already at the endpoint from the
beginning in the expanse of *dharmadhātu*. There is no entering into this
path through conceptual thought, nor traveling along it with effort. It is
crossing over in that it is beyond, such that without travel you stay [in
the realization]. The root text continues, "*Bodhicitta* is beyond [the differences of] schools of thought or vehicles." Because all schools of thought

and vehicles [represent ways of] grasping at partialities with conceptual thought by individuals, with respect to *bodhicitta*, from the very beginning there are no schools of thought, nor particular vehicles. It is crossing over in that it is beyond partiality and divisions. The root text continues, "[Forms of this] means that, with respect to abiding in the illusion of the seeming external world, there seem to exist [distinctions] such as good/bad, top/bottom, etc. However, with respect to staying in the expanse of *dharmadhātu*, there are no distinctions such as good/bad, top/bottom, etc. This is crossing over in that it is beyond the nine realms that are the expanse of *dharmadhātu*]."

Third, the conclusion is clearly expressed when the root text says, "This completes the nail of crossing over into sameness. *Samaya!*"

17: The Nail of Reaching the Endpoint, Being Victorious in the Embodiment of Enlightenment

Homage to Kun tu bZang po, who has reached the end [of the path] as the enlightened embodiment of the Victorious One. The four elements [dissolve] into the expanse of space, and the [seeming independent] world of appearance is [completely] exhausted. [At this point] the gateways [to the path], the vehicles, and the Bon tantras [all] are [completely] exhausted in the expanse of *dharmadhātu*. The mind and mental events are [completely] exhausted in the expanse of awakened mind-itself. The various particular [types of] actions [in meditation] are [completely] exhausted in the expanse of not-doing. Various expressions and talk are [completely] exhausted in the expanse of expressionlessness. The great accumulation of recollections and conceptual thoughts are [completely] exhausted in the expanse free of thought. The various paths resulting from the activity of conceptual thought are [completely] exhausted in the expanse that surpasses all conceptual thought. The various schools of thought, all of which hold partial views, are [completely] exhausted in the expanse without partiality. The three—ultimate sound, light, and light-rays—are [completely] exhausted in the expanse of awakened awareness. The entirety of *samsāra* and *nirvāna* is [completely] exhausted into *bodhicitta*. The visions, however, are not [completely] exhausted, and are neither stopped nor obstructed.

You reach the end wherein they become liberated at [the very point of just beginning to] occur. Unending, they manifest without obstruction in the three times unceasingly [as inexhaustible enlightened activity]. This completes the nail of reaching the endpoint. *Samaya!*

Seventeenth, the nail of reaching the endpoint has three parts, the first being the homage. The root text says, "Homage to Kun tu bZang po, who has reached the end [of the path] as the enlightened embodiment of the Victorious One." This passage explains the homage. This means that because *bodhicitta* is the full measure of everything, it is explained that there is nothing other that existed before.

Second, the extensive explanation is as follows: The root text begins, "The four elements [dissolve] into the expanse of space and the [seeming independent] world of appearance is [completely] exhausted." This means that all the elements and all of the [forms of the] seemingly existing world, as much as it is, reaches an end in the great emptiness/clarity of space. The root text continues, "[At this point] the gateways [to the path], the vehicles, and the Bon *tantras* [all] are completely exhausted in the expanse of *dharmadhātu*." This means that all the gateways of Bon, the vehicles, and the *tantras*, as much as there are, reach the end in the expanse of *dharmadhātu*. The root text continues, "The mind and mental events are [completely] exhausted in the expanse of awakened mind-itself." This means that awakened mind-itself is self-occurring primordial wisdom. The root text continues, "The various particular [types of] action [in meditation and the agents of these actions] are [completely] exhausted in the expanse of not-doing." This means that the various activities of the body, as many as there are, reach an end in the expanse, which is completely without doing anything in the mind. The root text continues, "Various expressions and talk come to an end in the expanse of expressionlessness." This means that all the expressions of speech, as much as they are, reach an end in the expanse which is completely expressionless in the mind. The root text continues, "The great accumulation of recollections and conceptual thoughts are [completely] exhausted in the expanse free of thought." This means that all the various recollections and conceptual thoughts, as much as they are, reach an end in the expanse, which is completely without thought in the mind. The root text continues, "The various paths resulting from the activity of conceptual thought are [completely] exhausted in the expanse that surpasses all conceptual thought." This means that all the paths, which are constructed by conceptual thought, such as the views, meditations, etc. reach an end in a state which completely surpasses thought in the mind. The root text continues, "The various schools of thought, all of which hold partial views, are [completely] exhausted in the expanse without partiality." (620) This means that all the schools of thought, as many as there are, reach an end in the expanse, which is free of one-sidedness and divisions in the mind. The root text continues, "The three—ultimate sound, light, and light-rays—are [completely] exhausted in the expanse of awakened awareness." This means that all the visions of ultimate sound, light, and light-rays reach an end in primordial wisdom's self-arising awakened awareness. The root text continues, "The entirety of *saṃsāra* and *nirvāṇa* is [completely] exhausted as *bodhicitta*." This means that all of the phenomena of *saṃsāra* and *nirvāṇa* reach an end as *bodhicitta*. The root text continues, "The visions, however, do not come to an end, and are neither cut off nor obstructed." This means that everything without exception in *saṃsāra* and *nirvāṇa* is exhausted as *bodhicitta*. Having become exhausted, they do not occur again. Having been cut off, they do not exist. Having been obstructed, they no longer continuously occur. If you were to ask, how can that be? The root text answers by saying, "You reach the end wherein they become liberated at [the very point of just beginning to] occur." This means that all phenomena of *saṃsāra* and *nirvāṇa* are touched by *bodhicitta*, both at the very beginning [of their existence at the source of their] coming into being, and also at their end in being liberated, and are thereby said to be exhausted. The root text continues, "Unending, they manifest without obstruction in the three times unceasingly [as inexhaustible enlightened activity]." This passage means that this magical display of *bodhicitta* [is actually] without exhaustion and comes into being everywhere. Because it is unobstructed, it arises in whatever ways, and so it is said to be without interruption in the three times.

Third, the conclusion is clearly expressed when the root text says, "This completes the nail of reaching the endpoint. *Samaya!*"

18: The Nail of Compassion that Protects Beings From the Jaws of Death

Homage to Kun tu bZang po, whose compassion protects all beings. (563) At the time of death the mind separates from the body, and the individual [finds himself] at the boundary of happy and miserable states. Those of best capacity are taught the pith instructions on self-arising primordial wisdom. They are offered the instructions on the sameness of all the various appearances [during the dying process]. [Through these instructions] they will come to see the true face of their identity [as awakened awareness]. There is no doubt. Those of middling capacity are taught the pith instructions about [these being] self-appearing illusions. They are offered the instructions to be without attachment or desire [to anything that appears in the dying process]. [Through these instructions] they close the gateways to [future] rebirths. There is no doubt. Those of lesser capacity are taught [to remember] the pith instructions of their tutelary deity (*yi dam*) and their [root] lama [while dying]. They are offered the instructions for [cultivating] interest, admiration, and respect. They will attain a happy [future] rebirth. There is no doubt.

This completes the nail of generating *bodhicitta* [when facing] the jaws of death. *Samaya!*

Eighteenth, the nail of generating *bodhicitta* in the jaws of death has three parts, the first of which is the homage. The root text begins, "Homage to Kun tu bZang po, whose compassion protects beings." This passage explains the homage. This shows how [sentient beings] are protected from the fears of *saṁsāra*.

Second, the extensive explanation is as follows: The root text begins, "At the time of death the mind separates from the body." This passage refers to impermanence and [specifically] to the time of dying. The root text continues, "and the individual [finds himself] at the boundary of happy and miserable states." This passage refers to the cross-road [encountered at the time of dying, leading either] upward to attaining a happy re-birth, or downward to falling into an unhappy re-birth. At that time, [the individual] is propelled by the [karmic] strength of good or bad thoughts, and there is a significant difference [in the direction taken]. Therefore, it is very important to have a [solid] foundation in the instructions.

The root text continues, "Those of best capacity are taught the special instructions on self-arising primordial wisdom." This means that, with respect to those of best capacity, the king of awakened awareness, self-arising primordial wisdom free of obscurations and coverings, is pointed out. The root text continues, "They are offered the instructions on the sameness of all the various appearances [during the dying process]." This means that the full measure of the visions and the full measure of arising are shown to be the same taste in the mind. "Through these instructions," as the root text says, "they will come to see the true face of their identity [as the king of awakened awareness]....There is no doubt."

The root text continues, "Those of middling capacity are taught the pith instructions about [these being] self-appearing illusions." This means that for the individual of middling capacity the full measure of the visions and the full measure of arising is shown to be existing as mind [only]. It is pointed out that all seeming appearances are illusory. The root text says, "They are offered the instructions to be without attachment or desire [to anything that appears in the dying process]." This means that they are taught not to become attached to or desirous of anything whatsoever. The root text says, "[Through these instructions] they close the gateways to [future] rebirths. There is no doubt." This means that through these instructions, there is no doubt that the gateways to re-birth in *saṃsāra* will close.

The root text continues, "Those of lesser capacity are taught [to remember] the pith instructions of their tutelary deity [*yi dam*] and lama." This means that with respect to those individuals of lesser capacity, they should be well established in meditation on their *yi dam* and with admiration and respect for their [root] lama [while dying]. (622) The root text continues, "They are offered the instructions for [cultivating] interest, admiration, and respect." This refers to making a request [for the gift-waves of influence] with admiration and respect for the holy lama. The root text ends by saying, "They will attain a happy rebirth. There is no doubt."

Third, the conclusion is clearly expressed in the root text when it says, "This completes the nail of generating *bodhicitta* [when facing] the jaws of death. S*amaya!*"

19: The Nail of Complete Self-Liberation and *Buddhahood* During the After-Death State

Homage to Kun to bZang po, who [represents] self-liberation, complete *Buddhahood*.

At the time [of the after-death states either] liberation or delusion is shown. The external elements dissolve in their own way. The internal elements remain latent [within the universal ground]. Various dualistic thoughts dissolve into the domain of space. At that time, awakened awareness stays nakedly, and self-occurring primordial wisdom is without covering or obscuration. Those few fortunate ones who have made a close-to-the-heart determination about this have torn asunder the three nets [appearance, conceptual thought, and the physical body], and have completed the three skills.

However, if there is no liberation at that time, then the first after-death state will arise. The light [that appears at this time represents] the pure realms without edges or middle, like a rainbow arising in the sky. Sound [that appears at this time represents] the insubstantial roar in the domain of space, very much the way thunder occurs by itself, continuously. Light-rays [that appear at this time, represent] an indefinite miraculous display, very much like unfurling a silken or woolen brocade.

For those individuals who are familiar with or acquainted with this, the enlightened bodies and the [entire array of the] *mandala* (564) arise as complete. At that time, the paranormal powers and the divine mindfulnesses arise. The three types of visions arise, but you are not bothered by them. Through your familiarity with them, you do not have to suppress them [but allow them to arise unobstructedly]. Once awakened awareness is integrated into your mind-stream, these [visions] are suppressed in the universal ground. Come to see the true face of these visions, much like seeing one's own face in a mirror. The true identity of awakened awareness comes to meet itself-by-itself, like a king who recognizes his own son. Not recognizing awakened awareness and delusion become purified in their own way, like the sun [shining] over an island that has been covered in the darkness. The king of awakened awareness ends up manifesting [at all times] in its own way, like the king's son who ends up in the original place of [his father's] kingdom.

The three—sound, light, and light-rays—become purified in the mind, like gathering droplets of the sun into the mother [sun]. The residual dregs become liberated as radiant purity in the domain of space, like ice melting in the ocean. The conditioned becomes calm in the state of the unconditioned, like salt dissolving in water. Karma and afflictive emotions become liberated in the [universal] ground, like all the clouds [evaporating] in a clear sky. Whatever is stirred from the depths of the three realms of samsāra is completely reversed, like water drying up in an irrigation channel. Samsāra and nirvāna, inseparable, become purified in the universal ground, like a rainbow disappearing in the sky. The mandalas and the three-fold embodiment of enlightenment arise in full strength, like the rays of the sun and a water-moon.

For those individuals who have only slight familiarity with this, the king of awakened awareness remains dormant. Once they have remained in this state for one to three days, by the seventh day the radiant purity [of the visions] gradually arises, but the pure realms do not arise as complete. If the conditions [are right], there can still be liberation in this bardo. If there is no liberation [at this time], the residual dregs of [impure] visions [begin to] arise. [It is still possible] to see pure visions during the [next] after-death state, the bardo of becoming, [and, in so doing,] to become emancipated quickly from this continuous unfolding [of re-births] into a favorable rebirth [in a pure realm].

Those individuals without the gateway to these instructions will

not recognize the clarity of the natural state. (565) They see [the after-death] visions as something other, as real appearances. They fall into the trap of delusion and wander [continuously] in *samsāra*. Because of that, fortunate ones make a close-to-the-heart determination [about delusion]. This completes the nail at the time of the after-death states. *Samaya!*

Nineteenth, the nail of the time of the after-death state has three parts, the first of which is the homage as the root text says, "Homage to Kun to bZang po, who [represents] self-liberation, complete *Buddhahood*." This passage explains the homage. This passage shows that if *bodhicitta* is realized, *Buddhahood* comes without [going through] the after-death states.

Second, the extensive explanation has two parts:

(1) A briefer explanation of liberation and delusion, and

(2) A more extensive explanation.

First, the briefer explanation is as follows: The root text begins, "At the time [of the after-death states, either] liberation or delusion is shown." This means that if there is realization at this time, there is liberation, and if there is no realization at this time, there is delusion. If you were to ask what time is this, the root text answers, "The external elements dissolve in their own way. The internal elements remain latent [within the universal ground]." This passage refers to the way the elements disintegrate and become absorbed [at the time of death]. This process has been elucidated in *The Six Essential Points of Bodhicitta*. The root text continues, "Various dualistic thoughts dissolve into the domain of space." This means that at the time the body and mind become separated, the grasped, the grasper [i.e., duality], and all the conceptual thoughts, dissolve into the domain of the universal ground. The root text continues, "At that time, awakened awareness stays nakedly, and self-occurring primordial wisdom is without covering or obscuration." This again refers to the time during death when the body and mind separate. At that time it is possible that either one's karma is pure or impure. All at once, there is separation from the body, which is an illusion, and all the conceptual thoughts of the mind, and all the obscurations and coverings of the sense-objects, (623) and the universal ground and awakened awareness [shine forth] like the sun free of darkness, or like a cloudless sky. All at once these stay without obscuration or coverings.

Second, the more detailed explanation has two parts:

(1) Showing the way of liberation, and

(2) Showing the way of delusion.

The first [showing the way of liberation] has three parts—for those of best, middling, and lesser capacity.

First, [for those of best capacity] the root text says, "Those few fortunate ones who have made a close-to-the-heart determination about this have torn asunder the three nets [appearance, conceptual thought, and the physical body], and have completed the three skills." This means that those individuals having confidence have given up the aggregates [of the physical body], torn apart the nets of the three gateways—body, speech, and mind—and have completed the three skills of enlightened body, speech, and heart-mind. They continuously act for the benefit of sentient beings.

Second, for those of middling capacity, the root text says, "However, if there is no liberation at that time, then the first after-death state will arise." This means that at the time [of death when] the body and mind separate, if there is no liberation at the very moment, one [nevertheless] stays in the natural state; and then, during the [next] after-death state [the after-death state of *dharmadhātu*], the clear-light of *dharmadhātu* arises. If you were to ask, how does this arise, at this very moment [the four elements]—fire, water, earth, and wind—and the seeming appearances of the external container and internal contents cease. Then, the three visions—ultimate sound, light, and light-rays arise. There are two [considerations]: the manner of arising, and the manner of liberation.

First, with respect to the manner of arising, the root text says, "The light [that appears at this time represents] the pure realms without edges or middle." This refers to the visions of the five lights arising without an above or below, without cardinal or intermediate direction, and without any center or edges. What metaphor best conveys this? The root text says, "like a rainbow arising in the sky." These five lights arise like a rainbow in the sky. (624) The root text continues, "Sound [that appears at this time represents] the insubstantial roar in the domain of space." This refers to the inherent sounds of emptiness in *dharmadhātu*. They are self-occurring sounds in the domain [of space] in the mind. If one were to ask, what is this like, the root text answers with the metaphor, "very much the way thunder occurs by itself, continuously." This refers to the way thunder is a continuous sound. The root text continues, "Light-rays [that appear at this time represent] an indefinite miraculous display." This means that such visions of the magical display of awakened awareness arise without doing anything. If one were to ask, what is this like, the root text answers, "very much like unfurling a silken or woolen brocade." This means that it is like opening a silken or woolen brocade.

How do they arise? The root text says, "For those individuals who are familiar with or acquainted with this, the enlightened bodies and the [entire array of the] *mandala* arise as complete." This refers to those who are familiar with and used to these instructions. Then, at this time in the dying process, the king of thumb-sized awakened awareness appears as an inherent body, as a light-body about the length of the distance between two arms stretched out. Moreover, the illusion of the [physical] body is not like this [light-body]. This light-body appears without front or back and without cardinal or intermediate directions. In the space of that [clear-light body], in all ten directions countless energy drops and offering tents of light appear. Within each and every one of these energy drops the five [lights like] an offering tent arise. Within the center of these five offering tent lights, each of the five enlightened *Buddhas* arise. These appear in the manner of clusters and rows. Furthermore, these enlightened bodies and the offering tent of lights do not arise from anywhere else. They arise from the inherent nature of awakened awareness. Furthermore, from the basis of arising of this thumb-sized enlightened body of light in the center of one's own physical heart, it arises like that in the ten directions of space. Furthermore, this physical heart is material. The visionary lights that arise from the physical heart are not material.

Second, with respect to the manner of liberation, the root text says,

"At that time, the paranormal powers and divine mindfulnesses arise." This means that when the six paranormal powers and the six types of extraordinary mindfulnesses arise, liberation follows. These six paranormal powers and six types of extraordinary mindfulnesses are elucidated in the *Six Essential Points of Bodhicitta*. The root text continues, "The three types of visions arise but you are not bothered by them." The three—ultimate sound, light, and light-rays—arise but not as any bother to awakened awareness, much like meeting with an old friend you have met before. The root text continues, "Through your familiarity with them, you do not have to suppress them [but allow them to arise unobstructedly]." If you carry on with them as was previously the case, the root text says, "Once awakened awareness is integrated into your mind-stream, these [visions] are suppressed in the universal ground. Come to see the true face of these visions." This means that at this very time the three visions—ultimate sound, light, and light-rays—and the visions of the enlightened bodies and energy drops arise in-and-by-themselves as the inherent face of one's own awakened awareness. This awakened awareness sees itself-by-itself. If one were to ask what is this like, the root text answers, "much like seeing one's own face in a mirror. The true identity of awakened awareness comes to meet-itself-by-itself." This means that through the activities of the conditions [associated with] the three visions, one's true identity, the king of awakened awareness, meets itself-by-itself. For example, it is like the occasion in which the son of a king wanders among the common people [yet is still recognized] as the king's son. That is why the root text says, "like the king who recognizes his own son." The root text continues, "Not recognizing awakened awareness and delusion become purified in their own way." This means that since the king of awakened awareness has been recognized, the darkness of the non-recognition of awakened awareness is purified again and again. The example in the root text to illustrate this is, "like the sun [shining] on an island that has been covered by darkness." The root text continues, "The king of awakened awareness ends up manifesting [at all times] in its own way." This means that at this time, since awakened awareness ends up in its own way, (626) it does not chase after the visions. The example in the root text to illustrate this is, "like the king's son who ends up in the original place [of his father's] kingdom."

The root text continues, "The three—sound, light, and light-rays—become purified in the mind." This means that at that point in time the three—ultimate sound, light, and light-rays—are brought together in the domain of space of the vast expanse and become liberated, as the root text says with the metaphor, "like gathering droplets of the sun into the mother [sun]." The text continues, "The residual dregs become liberated as radiant purity in the domain of space." This refers to the appearance [of the elements]—fire, water, earth, and wind. Since they are liberated in-and-by-themselves in the domain of space of the five elemental energy lights, these become liberated. The root text uses a metaphor to illustrate, "like ice melting in the ocean." The root text continues, "The conditioned becomes calm in the state of the unconditioned." This refers to the conditioned aggregate [of the physical body] that is an illusion. Since [this aggregate] has become calm-in-and-by-itself into the state of the unconditioned enlightened body and primordial wisdom energy, this becomes liberated. The text uses the metaphor to illustrate, "like salt dissolving in water." The root text continues, "Karma and afflictive emotions become liberated in the [universal] ground." This passage refers to the causes of *saṃsāra*, namely karmic traces and afflictive emotions. Since all of these have been liberated in-and-by-themselves directly in the natural state, the universal ground, these have become liberated. The root text uses the metaphor to illustrate, "like all the clouds [evaporating] in a clear sky." The root text continues, "Whatever is stirred from the depths of the three realms of *saṃsāra* is completely reversed." This means that since the causes [of *saṃsāra*], karmic traces and afflictive emotions, have been liberated-in-and-by-themselves, then also the effects, the depths of the sufferings of *saṃsāra* that have been stirred up, also are liberated in-and-by-themselves. The root text uses the metaphor to illustrate, "like water drying up in an irrigation channel," so there is no cause for the water to flow. The root text continues, "*Saṃsāra* and *nirvāṇa*, inseparable, become purified in the universal ground." This refers to all the characteristics of grasping at the duality of *saṃsāra* and *nirvāṇa*, which, having been purified-in-and-by-themselves in the natural state, the universal ground, have become liberated. The root text continues with a metaphor, "like a rainbow disappearing in the sky," to illustrate the [process of] liberation. The root text says, "The *mandalas* and the three-fold embodiment of enlightenment arise in full strength." This means that at this point in time (627) the Completion Body [*sambhogakāya*] arises in-and-by-itself from the liveliness of *dharmakāya*, and then the Emanation Bodies [*nirmāṇakāyas*] arise in-and-by-themselves from the liveliness of the Completion Body, and these [Emanation Bodies inexhaustibly] work for the benefit of sentient beings. The root text continues with a metaphor to illustrate, "like the rays of the sun and a water-moon."

Third, the way of liberation for those of lesser capacity is as follows: The root text begins, "For those individuals who have only slight familiarity with this, the king of awakened awareness remains dormant." This means that while such individuals may be taught these instructions they are likely to have little familiarity [with awakened awareness] and likely to be less intelligent. For them, the king of awakened awareness is dormant within the universal ground. They do not even know that they ultimately stay in the natural state, and thus do not stay the way a Victorious One [a *Buddha*] does. The root text continues, "Once they have remained in this state of one to three days [after-death]." This passage refers to how long awakened awareness remains dormant within the universal ground [after death]. It may remain one day. It may remain two days. It may remain three days. Yet, it may remain [this way] for just a brief instance or a short moment. The root text continues, "by the seventh day the radiant purity [of the visions] gradually arises." This means that from the first day until the seventh day, on each successive day in stages, first a white light, then a green light, a red light, a blue light, and [finally] a yellow light arises. The root text continues, "but the pure realms do not arise as complete." This means that due to the very little strength of familiarity, the enlightened bodies and *mandalas* do not arise as complete. Instead, only the three—ultimate sound, light, and light-rays—arise. The root text continues, "If the conditions [are right] there can still be liberation." This means that sometime thereafter [in a future re-birth], by behaving virtuously, by being taught the instructions by a lama, and by having received the prophecies of your tutelary deity (*yi dam*), liberation will [eventually come] in the after-death state of clear-light. The root text continues, "If there is no liberation [at this time], the residual dregs of [impure] visions [begin to] arise." (628) This means that if there is no liberation from that [at that point in the dying process], because the five radiant lights have become dormant, the residual dregs [of the four elements]—fire, water, earth, and wind—appear. The root text continues, "[It is still possible] to see pure visions during the after-death state of existence [or rebirth]." This means that by virtue of the after-death state of existence now having arisen from that [previous after-death clear-light state], because of the [residual] force of good karma, it is still possible to see some pure visions from the three—ultimate sound, light, and light-rays. The root text then says, "[and in so doing], to become emancipated quickly from this continuous unfolding [of rebirths] into a favorable rebirth [in a pure realm]." This means that [such an individual] will have a favorable re-birth, and the mind-stream [in the next life also] remains [in that favorable] re-birth and, in the end, remaining connected [over re-births] to the proliferation of [good] karma, liberation comes quickly [in some future re-birth].

Second, showing the way of delusion begins with the root text stating, "Those individuals without the gateway to these instructions will not recognize the clarity of the natural state." This refers to those individuals who have not entered the gateway of these instructions in a reliable manner. For them, at the time of death, when the body and mind become separated and they remain in the [after-death] state of clear-light, they fail to recognize the lucidity of the natural state, even when it is free of obscurations and coverings. The root text continues, "They see [the after-death] visions as something other, as real appearances." This means that in the after-death state of clear-light, they do not even know the three visions—ultimate sound, light, and light-rays—as appearing in-and-by-themselves. They see these as appearing out there, and as existing beyond their own mind-stream. The root text continues, "They fall into the trap of delusion and wander [continuously] in *saṁsāra*." This means that in the [subsequent] after-death state of existence or rebirth, since only deluded appearances of the three—ultimate sound, light, and light-rays—have arisen, then the causes of *saṁsāra* are re-created, and they wander [aimlessly] in *saṁsāra*. The root text continues, "Because of that, fortunate ones make a close-to-the-heart determination [about delusion]." This means that because both liberation and delusion are quite distinct from each other, hereafter, fortunate individuals [with the right karmic connection] make a decisive close-to-the-heart determination at this very moment [while they still can].

Third, the conclusion is clearly expressed when the root text says, "This completes the nail at the time of the after-death state. *Samaya!*"

20: The Nail that Eliminates the Extremes of Mistaken Ideas

Homage to Kun tu bZang po, who eliminates the darkness of mistaken ideas.

These are the instructions about the essential points for reaching the end [of the path]. There are those who do not have [the right] karmic connection and good fortune. They are without the [proper] vessel. If they come to the instructions, some will grasp after a self. They are mistaken in grasping eternalism and staying in extreme non-Buddhist views. Others proclaim that the visions do not exist. They are mistaken in staying in nihilism and getting rid of things. Others cling to [a view] of something supreme. They are mistaken and will get a rebirth in the long-lasting realm [of the gods]. Others are full of conceit. They are locked in the chains of grasping an "I" and what they know. Others grasp things as real, and because of becoming attached to grasping things as real they are bound to *samsāra*. Others remain panicked or afraid. They are mistaken in that they remain in the lower vehicles for those of lesser intellect. Others get caught up in criticizing these venerated [teachings]. They will not meet with ultimate truth for eons and it will take them much longer than expected. Others get all mixed up about the oral instructions. Because they have let their spiritual duties degenerate they will fall into a bad existence, and thus into the great abyss [of *samsāra*]. Therefore, these sacred special instructions should be concealed in the treasury of mind in the universal ground. Without spreading [these instructions widely] they must be sealed as secret. This completes the nail that purifies the extremes of mistaken ideas. *Samaya!*

Twentieth, the nail that eliminates the extremes of mistaken ideas has three parts, the first of which is the homage, as expressed in the root text, "Homage to Kun tu bZang po, who eliminates the darkness of mistaken ideas." This passage explains the homage. This means that through having made a decisive determination using these instructions, so that the ultimate truth of *bodhicitta* has been realized, then the darkness of mistaken ideas is purified in-and-by-itself.

Second, the extensive explanation begins with the root text stating, "These are the instructions about the essential points for reaching the end [of the path]. There are those who do not have [the right] karmic connection and good fortune. They are without the [proper] vessel." This means that if these instructions which set forth the essential points about awakened awareness are taught to anyone not having [the right] karmic connection and having good fortune, and to those without the proper vessel, then the fact that they do not realize the natural state is beyond [belief] and they will come to go astray on the wrong path. If you were to ask why is this so extraordinary, the root text answers by saying, "If they come to the instructions, some will grasp after a self. They are mistaken in grasping eternalism and staying in extreme non-*Buddhist* views." This means that if these instructions are taught about the three visions—ultimate sound, light, and light-rays—to those of little intelligence, then such individuals will grasp after a permanent self in their own mind-streams. Through the fault of this they will go astray like the non-*Buddhist* adherents of eternalism. The root text continues, "Others proclaim that the visions do not exist. They are mistaken in staying in nihilism and getting rid of things." This passage refers to other individuals also with little intelligence [who believe] that the mind is not a real thing, and also say that the three [visions]—ultimate sound, light, and light-rays—are untrue. Through the fault of this they will go astray to the extreme of nihilism and getting rid of things. The root text continues, "Others cling to [a view] of something supreme. They are mistaken and will get a rebirth in the long-lasting realm [of the gods]." (630) This passage refers to other individuals, also with little intelligence, who become attached to the three visions and grasp after them as a solid, ultimate realty. Through the fault of this they will go astray [to a re-birth] to the gods with long lives. The root text continues, "Others are full of conceit. They are locked in the chains of grasping an 'I' and what they know." This passage refers to other individuals, also with little intelligence who, although they see the three visions, are filled with a conceited pride. Through the fault of this they become bound by the obscurations of what they know. The root text continues, "Others grasp things as real, and because of becoming attached to grasping things as real they are bound to *saṃsāra*." This passage refers to other individuals, also with little intelligence, who through grasping the three visions as real and having [solid] characteristics, through the fault of this, they are destined to remain in *saṃsāra* and thereafter return [over and over]. The root text continues, "Others remain panicked or afraid. They are mistaken in that they stay in a lower vehicle for those of lesser intellect." These special instructions are not fit for some individuals of little intelligence and so they become afraid. Through the fault of this they will go astray like the Hearers [*Shravakas*] of the lower vehicles. The root text continues, "Others get caught up in criticizing these venerated [teachings]. They will not meet with ultimate truth for eons and it will take them much longer than expected." This refers to some individuals who say that these pith instructions are untrue and therefore criticize them. Through the fault of this they will not meet with the ultimate truth of the natural state for eons. The root text continues, "Others get all mixed up about the oral instructions. Because they have let their spiritual duties degenerate they will fall into a bad existence, and thus into the great abyss [of *saṃsāra*]." This passage refers to some individuals who are entrusted with these pith instructions who do not have the proper vessel. Through the fault of this, their spiritual duties to the secret *mantra* practices have degenerated, and therefore they will fall into bad re-births.

Therefore, with respect to this [teaching these instructions], [you stand at the edge of] a great abyss. The root text says, "Therefore, these sacred special instructions should be concealed in the treasury of mind in the universal ground. Without spreading [these instructions widely] they must be sealed as a secret." This passage means that if [these instructions] are taught to those without a proper vessel, there are many ways to go astray thereafter. Therefore, the seal of secrecy should be affixed to these instructions.

Third, the conclusion is clearly expressed in the root text when it says, "This completes the nail that purifies the extremes of mistaken ideas. *Samaya!*"

21: The Nail of Realizing the Three Enlightened Bodies Directly, the Fruition

Homage to Kun tu bZang po, who is the direct manifestation of the three-fold embodiment of enlightenment. (566) Those who make a close-to-the-heart determination about the ultimate truth, without doubt, reach the end, and have the fruition occur. Because they made a close-to-the-heart determination about the universal ground, *samsāra* or *nirvāna* are swept away. Because they made a close-to-the-heart determination about awakened awareness, they remain completely purified of obscuration and delusion. Because they made a close-to-the-heart determination about conceptual thought, primordial wisdom has arisen as liveliness. Because they made a close-to-the-heart determination about the basis of delusion, they never turn away from awakened awareness after that.

By afflictive emotions brought to the place of becoming [fully] exhausted, the flow of *samsāra* is completely disrupted. By all paths becoming exhausted, you come to a state of great bliss. By all schools of thought [representing] one's own or others' views being brought to the place of becoming [fully] exhausted, there is no one-sidedness or partiality. By the elements brought to the place of becoming [fully] exhausted, you do not disappear into space. By the attributes [of the existing world] being brought to the place of becoming [fully] exhausted, you will not transfer or transform [consciousness] within the expanse. By sentient beings brought to the place of becoming [fully] exhausted, the mind becomes free of birth or death. By the three gateways brought to the place of becoming [fully] exhausted, the three livelinesses become complete with respect to the body. By the three visions brought to the place of becoming [fully] exhausted, the three kinds of *mandalas* arise.

Because the two expanses arise in you, there is the bliss of remaining in the *dharmadhātu*. Because the two lights arise in you, there is the bliss that is without end or limit. Because the eternal enlightened bodies have arisen in you, you become free of the enemy of unhappiness. Because the six divine eyes have arisen within you, nothing whatsoever can obscure this. Because the three-fold embodiment of enlightenment has arisen in you, the fruition comes, free of expectation of gain or fear of not getting it. Because of opening the gateway to the treasury of mind, whatever is needed becomes complete in itself. This completes the nail of directly manifesting the fruition. *Samaya!*

Twenty-first, the nail of directly manifesting fruition, has three parts, the first of which is the homage, and stated in the root text, "Homage to Kun tu bZang po, who is the direct manifestation of the three-fold embodiment of enlightenment." This passage explains the homage. This means that *bodhicitta* becomes fully manifest as the fruition [of the path].

Second, the extensive explanation has two parts—a brief explanation, and a more detailed explanation.

First, the brief explanation begins with the root text saying, "Those who make a close-to-the-heart determination about the ultimate truth, without doubt, reach the end, and have the fruition occur." This passage refers to those who have practiced with these instructions, and through them have made a decisive determination about the ultimate truth, and will have attained the fruition, which is explained subsequently, without hope of getting anything or fear of not getting it.

Second, the more detailed explanation is as follows: "Because they made a close-to-the-heart determination about the universal ground, *saṃsāra* and *nirvāṇa* are swept away." Since these instructions are the way to penetrate the universal ground, they [are the way] to make a decisive determination about the natural state of the universal ground, then, from all the characteristics of grasping *saṃsāra* and *nirvāṇa* as a duality having become liberated in-and-by-themselves, there is liberation. The root text continues, "Because they made a close-to-the-heart determination about awakened awareness, they remain completely purified of obscuration and delusion." This means that since there has been a decisive determination about the natural state of awakened awareness, (632) then there is purification in-and-by-itself of the darkness of delusion and obscuration without having to let anything go, and it goes on from here. The root text continues, "Because they made a close-to-the-heart determination about conceptual thought, primordial wisdom has arisen as liveliness." This means that since there has been a decisive determination about the natural state of conceptual thought, then all recollections and conceptual thoughts arise as the liveliness of self-occurring primordial wisdom. The root text continues, "Because they made a close-to-the-heart determination about the basis of delusion, they never turn away from awakened awareness after that." This means that since there has been a decisive determination about the natural state of the three visions—ultimate sound, light, and light-rays—[as the potential] basis for delusion, then it is no longer possible for awakened awareness to become deluded throughout the places of *saṃsāra*. The root text continues, "By afflictive emotions brought to a place of becoming [fully] exhausted, the flow of *saṃsāra* is completely disrupted." This means that since the causes of afflictive emotions have become exhausted directly into the natural state of the universal ground, the outcome is that the flow of *saṃsāra* in one's own mind-stream becomes dried up. The root text continues, "By all paths becoming exhausted you come to a state of great bliss." This means that since one has directly encountered the natural state of the universal ground, which is the penetration of all paths, then one comes to stay in the *dharmadhātu*, and there is nowhere else to go. The root text continues, "By all schools of thought [representing] one's own or others' views being brought to a place of becoming [fully] exhausted, there is no one-sidedness or partiality." This means that since one has directly encountered the natural state of the universal ground, which penetrates all schools of thought, then there is liberation in-and-by-itself of all the features through which various partialities of schools of thought have been held. The root text continues, "By the elements brought to a place of becoming [fully] exhausted, you do not disappear into space." This means that since one has directly encountered the natural state of the universal ground, which penetrates the five elements, then, even though the five elements have dissolved, the awakened mind-itself does not dissolve into the space of primordial wisdom. The root text continues, "By the attributes [of the existing world] being brought to a place of becoming [fully] exhausted, you will not transfer or transform [consciousness] within the expanse." This means that since one has directly encountered the natural state of the universal ground, which penetrates all appearances that have phenomenal characteristics, (633) then, although consciousness may seem to transfer with respect to these characteristics, [actually] there is no consciousness-transference with respect to awakened mind-itself. The root text continues, "By sentient beings brought to a place of becoming [fully] exhausted, the mind becomes free of birth and death." This means that since one has directly encountered the natural state of the universal ground, which penetrates [the nature of] sentient beings, although there may seem to be birth and death with respect to the [physical] body, there is no birth or death with respect to primordial wisdom's awakened awareness. The root text continues, "By the three gateways brought to a place of becoming [fully] exhausted, the three livelinesses become complete with respect to the body." This means that since one has directly encountered the natural state of the universal ground, which penetrates the three [gateways] of [ordinary] body, speech, and mind, then the three livelinesses of enlightened body, speech, and heart-mind arise, arising in-and-by-themselves. The root text continues, "By the three visions brought to a place of becoming [fully] exhausted, the three kinds of *mandalas* arise." This means that since one has directly encountered the natural state of the universal ground, which penetrates the three [visions] —ultimate sound, light, and light-rays—then, with respect to light, the visions arise as the enlightened body *mandala*, with respect to ultimate sound, the visions arise as the enlightened speech *mandala*, and with respect to light-rays, the visions arise as the enlightened omniscient heart-mind *mandala*. The root text continues, "Because the two expanses arise in oneself, there is the bliss of remaining in the *dharmadhātu*." This means that because the two [expanses]—the expanse of the universal ground, and the expanse of the visions—both arise in one's own mind, it is not necessary to seek another expanse elsewhere, and there is the bliss of staying in one's own place. The root text continues, "Because the two lights arise in yourself,

there is the bliss that is without end or limit." This means that because
the two lights—the light of primordial wisdom energy and the light of
the visions—both arise in your own mind, with respect to the light of
your own mind, there is no concern of this getting lost in the three times.
The root text continues, "Because the eternal enlightened bodies have
arisen in you, one is free of the enemy of unhappiness." This means that
because the immutable, eternal [ultimate reality] has arisen in your own
mind, (634) it can't be stopped by any kind of adverse conditions. The
root text continues, "Because the six divine eyes of Bon have arisen within you, nothing whatsoever can obscure this." This means that because
the six divine eyes have arisen in one's own mind, there is no longer
any fear of it being obscured by external or internal darkness. The root
text continues, "Because the three-fold embodiment of enlightenment
has arisen in you, the fruition comes free of expectation of gain or fear
of not getting it." This means that because the fruition, the three-fold
embodiment of enlightenment has arisen in one's own mind, there is
no hope of finding it somewhere else, and no fear of not getting it. The
root text continues, "Because of opening the gateway to the treasury of
mind, whatever is needed becomes complete in itself." This means that
because of opening the gateway of the treasury of awakened awareness,
one penetrates the treasury of the universal ground, and then all the
positive qualities of the nine needs occur in one's own mind.

Third, the conclusion is clearly expressed in the root text when it
says, "This completes the nail of directly manifesting the fruition. *Samaya!*"

This is the vital essence of all the oral readings and pith instructions.
It is the vehicle that brings the end of all the paths, and the epitome of
all the vehicles, the oral lineage of the great masters [*Mahāsattvas*], the
final attainment of all those fortunate ones. (567)

This completes the essential points regarding the twenty-one nails. It
has been transmitted along a successive lineage of all the previous great
masters through whom [the teachings] have spread.

Sarvamangalam!

(634) Third, with respect to the conclusion of the [commentary], the root text says, "This is the vital essence of all the *tantras*, oral readings, and special instructions. It is the final vehicle of all of the paths, and the epitome of all the vehicles, the oral lineage of the great masters [*mahā-sattvas*], the attainment of all those fortunate ones. (567) This completes the essential points regarding the twenty-one nails propagated along a successive lineage of all the previous great masters." This passage gives the conclusion.

This commentary to the twenty-one nails, which explains the way to penetrate the very secret nature of the natural state, made by gYer spungs sNang bzher Lod bo, is completed.

Bibliography

A. Tibetan Works Used:

rDzogs pa chen po zhang zhung snyan rgyud las gzer bu nyi shu rtsa gcig gi gzhung bzhugs so, Bon Dialectic School, Menri Monastery, Solan, HP, India, 2010, pp. 550-567.

rDzogs pa chen po zhang zhung snyan rgyud las gzer bu nyer gcig gi 'grel pa gzhugs so, Bon Dialectic School, Menri Monastery, Solan, HP, India, 2010, pp. 568-634.

B. Western Works:

Lopon Tenzin Namdak, Tenzin Wangyal Rinpoche, & Klein, Anne. (1996). *Twenty-One Nails. Vol. II. Oral commentary,* A. Jones & S. Tainer (Eds.).

Reynolds, John Myrdhin. (2014). *The Precepts of the Dharmakaya: Translation of The Twenty-One Little Nails—The Root Text and its Commentary from the Zhang Zhung Tradition of Tibet,* Kathmandu, Nepal: Vajra Books.

Tenzin Wangyal Rinpoche, Keutzer, K. (2002-2003). *The Twenty-One Nails: A Dzogchen Text from the Oral Transmission of Zhang Zhung. Vol. 73, International Academy of Indian Culture,* New Delhi, India.

Printed in the USA
CPSIA information can be obtained
at www.ICGtesting.com
LVHW022318081223
765728LV00031B/568/J